# Syntactical Mechanics

OKLAHOMA SERIES IN CLASSICAL CULTURE

# Syntactical Mechanics

*A New Approach to English, Latin, and Greek*

*Bruce A. McMenomy*

UNIVERSITY OF OKLAHOMA PRESS : NORMAN

LIBRARY OF CONGRESS CATALOGING-IN-PUBLICATION DATA

McMenomy, Bruce Alan, 1954– author.
Syntactical mechanics : a new approach to English, Latin, and Greek /
Bruce A. McMenomy.
    pages cm — (Oklahoma series in classical culture ; volume 51)
ISBN 978-0-8061-4494-8 (pbk. : alk. paper) 1. Latin language—Syntax.
2. Greek language—Syntax. 3. English language—Syntax. I. Title.
II. Series: Oklahoma series in classical culture ; v. 51.
PA2285.M37 2014
485—dc23
                                        2014001230


*Syntactical Mechanics: A New Approach to English, Latin, and Greek*
is Volume 51 in the Oklahoma Series in Classical Culture.

For my family, who understood.

*Christe, Mary, David, and Sarah*

# Contents

# Figures

# Preface

This book is an outgrowth of a need I have perceived for a number of years as a teacher of Latin and Greek. The philological teaching of Latin and Greek has always been largely about grappling with grammar. There are those who consider that method unrealistic, outdated, or backward, and who favor teaching classical languages using the inductive principles more commonly used for modern languages. But whether one learns Latin and Greek by an immersive inductive method or by a deductive and analytic one, certainly one of the real benefits of studying them is an organic sense of grammar per se—not just the particular grammar of the language in question, but a deeper sense of how grammar at all levels shapes, contextualizes, and mediates meaning. This book is largely about that connection.

I have long believed that in order for any kind of language instruction to work, it must ultimately be rooted in an awareness that syntactical structures, for all their variety and apparent fussiness, exist entirely for the sake of serving the speaker's meaning. It is not enough for a Latinist to master a list of ablative constructions: it is important to know how they work—that is, why they actually mean what they mean. This kind of understanding will eventually also involve an awareness of where the constructions came from, and how they came to function as they do. An organic mastery of the Latin ablative requires that one understand that it is not really one case, but a composite of two: a true ablative (separative) and an instrumental case. This is not mere historical trivia; it is part of the meaning of those constructions.

So armed, moreover, a Latinist first encountering Greek (or the Hellenist first encountering Latin) will find the apparent inconsistencies between the two languages far less daunting. If one knows how the Proto-Indo-European cases were distributed among the two languages, it makes sense that certain Latin ablative constructions emerge in Greek in the genitive, while others appear in Greek in the dative. Of those, I would argue, the former are genuinely ablatival, while the latter presuppose an instrumental origin and concept. This can shape how we understand them.

Linguistic exploration of this sort is often considered the province of graduate students and professional linguists. For some, it may be so. For me, this kind of synthesis would have smoothed the earlier path considerably. This, then, is the book I might have wished for, had I even speculated on its possibility, when I was first struggling with Latin, and (even more) when I moved from Latin to Greek. It contains, as far as I know, no new research, and probably tells the expert nothing new. Neither does it presume to be exhaustive. It is an attempt to provide the intermediate student with an overview of the lay of the land, and a way of thinking about syntax. It is not a systematic syntax of any language, and it deals with morphology almost not at all. It deals with syntax broadly—too broadly, some will surely argue—primarily as a gateway to semantics. If it helps form that awareness in even a few newer students, it will have done its job.

I would argue, finally, that in this light, the traditional deductive approach to the study of Latin and Greek draws at least a bit closer to the more contemporary inductive approaches. Ultimately both are about helping students achieve a synthetic understanding, rather than just a raw cataloging of disjunct grammatical phenomena.

In writing this book, I have of course been helped by many people and by many books. The latter I have tried to sketch in a bibliography, but it is highly likely that there are many books whose influence can be felt but which I have forgotten, at least at the conscious level. To their authors, living or dead, I apologize.

Of the people, most particular thanks are due to Ronnie Ancona, whose thoughtful suggestions and persistent encouragement prompted me to push this project forward into something that might reach a wider audience, and whose ongoing advice kept me on track when I was befuddled or simply weary of it all.

More generally, I must thank the extraordinary students in my Latin and Greek classes at Scholars Online, without whom this book would never have been imagined or created. In addition I should acknowledge Rachel Ahern Knudsen, who taught from the first murky versions of this material in a course during the summer of 2006. Thanks as well must go many other friends and former students who encouraged me to push ahead with this project, and in particular to my daughter Mary McMenomy (an accomplished classicist in her own right and one of my own first students), and especially to my wife, Christe McMenomy, whose love and support exceed my powers of description.

# Syntactical Mechanics

# CHAPTER 1

# The Eight Parts of Speech—
# All Eleven of Them

*Robust functional definitions, together with useful suggestions
concerning which eight you should pick for any occasion*

If you were taught the rudiments of grammar the way most people were taught fifty to a hundred years ago, you probably learned the eight parts of speech. The system was probably also presented as something near to revealed truth, and beyond question, as if set in stone from the foundation of the world. A noun is a noun is a noun, and that's all there is to it. Most people learned to intone, "A noun is the name of a person, place, or thing," and something similar (with more or less certainty) for each of the remaining parts of speech.

The ancient world knew about eight parts of speech, too, so it seems that it should be simple to line them up . . . but it's not. As it turns out, while the parts of speech are pretty basic, some are more basic than others, and at different times in the history of Western languages, their definitional boundaries have shifted.

Figure 1 distinguishes eleven different part-of-speech *functions* (down the

**Fig. 1.** Parts of Speech

| Modern | FUNCTION | Ancient |
|---|---|---|
| Pronoun | PRONOUN | Pronoun |
| Noun | SUBSTANTIVE | Noun |
| Adjective | STATIC ADJECTIVE | |
| | ACTIVE ADJECTIVE | Participle |
| | ARTICLE | Article |
| Preposition | PREPOSITION | Adverb (~Preposition) |
| Adverb | ADVERB | |
| Verb | VERB | Verb |
| Conjunction | CONJUNCTION | Ancient |
| Interjection | INTERJECTION | Interjection |
| | PARTICLE | Particle |

3

middle), and shows (in the left-hand column) what you probably learned to call them. If you've never heard of particles, that's okay. Most people haven't unless they've studied Greek or linguistics. (We're talking about particles as parts of speech—nothing to do with physical granular matter or with quantum mechanics.) We usually say that an article is an adjective, and that a participle is an adjective too, unless we are thinking of the fact that it came from a verb, in which case all bets are off.

The right-hand column contains the names given to these functions by ancient grammarians. (Actually they used Greek or Latin names, but these translations are reasonably accurate.) All of them were known in one way or another, but the interjection (grayed out) was not always thought of as a part of speech in ancient grammatical thinking.

What makes this interesting is that each system actually makes sense, and one can come to understand each system better through a synthetic vision of both.

## Names

The word "noun" comes to us through French *nom*, which in turn derived from the Latin *nomen*, which is not derived from, but has a common ancestry with, the Greek word ὄνομα (*onoma*), "name."

In English grammar we tend to distinguish *proper* nouns from *improper* or *common* nouns. The first thing we should get out of the way is any prejudice against those improper nouns. They're not any less well behaved than the others. They're just called *improper* because they're not *proper*, and that idea of propriety ("properness") comes from the Latin *proprius*, which means something like "specifically one's own" or "characteristic of someone or something in particular." It later came to refer to correct behavior, because proper behavior was the way one should be able to expect you to act—and hence what was improper had to do instead with getting out of your own place (whether that was one's social station or what my mother used to call "getting too big for your britches").

All of which is interesting, but the important point is that idea of something being *specifically one's own*. Proper nouns are those that belong to some *particular* referent—presumably what we would call a "name" in the narrow sense of the term. Here are some proper nouns:

| | | |
|---|---|---|
| Fred | Thomas Jefferson | United States of America |
| Narnia | Seattle Mariners | HTML |
| Microsoft Word | Apple Macintosh | Main Street |

We usually capitalize proper nouns in English, and it's customary to do so in Greek and Latin as well (though that's modern editorial practice—nothing to do with the way they were written in ancient manuscripts). There are a few things to note about proper nouns. First, while their referents are implicitly unique, they don't really have to be. That is, while *you* use them usually to refer to some particular person, place, thing, or idea, it's not guaranteed that other people will understand the same thing by those terms. If I refer to "Fred" without any last name in one group of my friends, everyone will understand which Fred I'm talking about, but there are other Freds in the world—a lot of them—and in a different group others might think I'm talking about someone else. If I talk about the Seattle Mariners, that's probably unambiguous. If I talk about Main Street, I'm probably talking about Main Street in my own city, but if I'm visiting somewhere else, I could be referring to the Main Street there. Many towns and cities have a Main Street, so context is important. Still, when I say "Main Street," it's usually going to be assumed that I'm talking about a *particular* Main Street, not about all streets that are "main" by virtue of running down the middle of town, or even those that are named "Main."

The use of the proper noun is also completely unaffected by the actual existence of something. If I refer to Thomas Jefferson, I'm doing so now that he's dead the same way I might have while he was alive. That is, the *referent* of the term remains the same. I can just as well refer to Narnia or Middle-earth, while remaining fully aware that both are fantasy creations (with apologies to those who find that disappointing). The chief distinction in proper nouns is that they are understood to refer to one thing, at least at the time of referring. Therefore ambiguity is generally at odds with using a proper noun. If you can't use it unambiguously (so that everyone who is hearing or reading your words will know what it means), you risk being misunderstood. Sometimes this is desirable, but in general it's not what you want to be doing.

*Improper* or *common* nouns are those that refer to things more generally, without requiring (necessarily) that people know which referent among several theoretical possibilities is under discussion. Here are some improper nouns:

| | | |
|---|---|---|
| banana | hyperbole | woman |
| table | dog | leg |
| poem | contradiction | triangle |
| canal | country | patriot |

Note that this list takes in the full range of persons (woman, patriot), places (canal, country), and things (banana, table, leg, contradiction, etc.). Improper nouns are just as capable of referring to persons, places, and things as proper nouns are. The difference here is that "woman" is not the given *name* of any particular woman, but a reference to a member of the class of women, just as "leg" is not a reference to any given leg—indeed, it could be a leg belonging to a woman, a dog, a table, or a triangle (also, by a contrived coincidence, items on this list). Even more than with proper nouns, context hugely influences the meaning of a common noun. A woman's leg is very little like a dog's, though they accomplish something of the same function; it's a lot less like a table leg, and the leg of a triangle (we only talk about "legs" in right triangles) is more or less an abstraction.

This brings us to another matter. So far we've noticed a major distinction that needs to be elaborated. We have included in our lists both *concrete* nouns and *abstract* nouns. Here are some examples of concrete nouns:

| Fred | Thomas Jefferson | Narnia |
|------|------------------|--------|
| banana | woman | table |
| dog | canal | |

These are considered *concrete* not because they were mixed up with cement and poured out into a mold, or because my friend Fred is a particularly stony fellow (he's a rock in a metaphorical sense, but we'll leave it at that), but because they all refer to *tangible* things—that is, *physical* things that can be touched. This is a great definition until you try to use it. For while I can touch a given table or dog, some of the things on that list are not *practically* touchable—Thomas Jefferson's remains could probably be dug up, but I don't particularly want to, and if I did so, I wouldn't really have hold of Thomas Jefferson himself anyway.

Narnia is an even tougher case. It's a fantasy world (or a country therein— there's some ambiguity in how it's used), but no matter how many wardrobes I bash through, I never seem to be able to reach any part of it physically. Still, we would normally consider it a tangible thing in the range of its own reference—i.e., if you really *were* there, you could touch it—and so we consider it a concrete noun.

*Abstract* nouns refer to things we *can't* touch, and couldn't ever understand how to touch in a mechanical sense. Here are some abstract nouns:

| HTML | Latin | love |
|------|-------|------|
| hyperbole | contradiction | |

We lump these together as abstract because they are of a *kind* not to be touched. This doesn't mean that they're any less *real* than concrete nouns. They are *called* "abstract" from the Latin verb *abstraho*, which means "draw out"—that is, they are ideas *taken from* something. There are some serious philosophical questions about where all this comes from, and whether these things we talk about as abstract are really drawn-out things or whether they come into the picture from elsewhere.

Plato and Aristotle began a fine old disagreement about that point—Plato arguing that *goodness* in things came into our physical reality because it *took part* in an out-there-somewhere Idea or Ideal of The Good. Aristotle argued that we form ideas like goodness or blueness or triangularity by seeing things in the real world that are good or blue or triangular. Clever people have disagreed for a long time about the difference between these two points of view, and if you find this question intriguing, I certainly recommend that you read some Plato and some Aristotle. In the meantime, however, it will probably suffice to note that, at least when it comes to talking about grammar, Aristotle effectively won the contest of terminologies—which is why we talk about these things generally as "abstract."

And then there are those cases that really sit astride the line between abstract and concrete nouns. What do we do about something like "the United States of America"? Does the name refer to the physical land? If so, it's concrete. Is it instead the idea or the form of government established in a portion of a particular continent for a time? If so, it's probably abstract. Is it the people who make it up? That would seem to be more concrete. If all the citizens of the United States were transported to a colony on Mars, would they still constitute the United States? We can continue this way virtually ad infinitum.

The point is that these classifying terms are ultimately terms of convenience. They are useful, but they are not absolutes, and there are different ways of looking at them. We will probably all agree to talk about some things as concrete and some things as abstract, but we'll probably also disagree about some others.

So far we've been talking about the kind of name that refers to something as a thing in and of itself, whether it's abstract or concrete. Now, here is one of the great divisions between ancient thinking on grammar and modern thought. Neither is particularly more correct than the other, but it helps to see the problem from both sides. Ancient grammarians would have classified the things we've been listing above as *substantives*. That is, they refer to what Aristotle (the first of the great philosophical grammarians) considered as having substance. This is not necessarily *physical* substance (i.e., matter, or what he called *hypokeimenon*). But it's the idea that there's *something* there that counts.

Ancient grammarians also, however, considered words that merely *described* things to be names for those things as well—words that we consider *adjectives*. You are probably already familiar with adjectives. Here are some examples:

| | | |
|---|---|---|
| gray | noble | elliptical |
| random | good | wise |
| slippery | | |

Possibly you haven't thought about adjectives much. An *adjective* is so called as a kind of short form of the original term "adjective noun"—Latin *nomen adiectivum*—which means that it's a name "thrown at" something. This probably doesn't make a whole lot of sense, since it's highly likely you haven't thrown any adjectives around in the recent past. It is perhaps a little more understandable as a translation of the Greek ὄνομα ἐπίθετον (*onoma epitheton*), which means "name put on or added to [something]." Yes, *epitheton* also makes a separate appearance in English as "epithet," which is used to describe formulaic adjectives like "swift-footed" in Homer (referring to Achilles), or, more recently, to describe usually disparaging adjectives thrown at people. It's unfortunate that a term with such a noble heritage has come to be used primarily to refer to racial slurs and the like. Either way, though, an epithet is really just an adjective. A nasty epithet is a nasty adjective, though the term has been muddied yet further in popular diction by the inclusion of nasty nouns as well.

While they did understand the distinction between the two, therefore, ancient grammarians tended to think of *substantive nouns* and *adjective nouns* as being broadly the same kind of thing. There are several reasons for this, some of them philosophical, and some of them accidents (if there are such things) of the languages they were speaking. It enabled them to talk about such things as "the names of God," where those names might include things we'd consider adjectives, like "good" and "wise." In English we might say: "I would call Fred wise"; but we probably wouldn't say: "I would *name* Fred wise" (unless his name happened to be Fred Wise, but it's not).

This makes a certain amount of sense. In usage, the barrier separating substantives and adjectives is tissue-thin. In Greek, Latin, and English alike, we can (pretty much at whim) *substantivize* any given adjective—that is, "promote" it to the status of a substantive, such that it can serve as the subject of a sentence or the object of a verb or a preposition without any further fuss and bother, as in these examples:

> the land of **the free**, and the home of **the brave**

and

> **The good** die young.

We understand that in these examples, "the free," "the brave," and "the good" refer to free people, brave people, and good people. We seldom think twice about using adjectives as subtantives this way, though there are some rare occasions on which it can lead to confusion.

Another reason ancient grammarians took adjectives and substantives together as types of nouns is that both Greek and Latin treated them in largely the same ways. There are differences between the classes of nouns and the classes of adjectives, but when one goes about inflecting these words—that is, tacking on the endings that tell us what their functions will be—these endings look very similar. While there are exceptions (quite a lot of them), there is a *tendency* for Greek and Latin nouns and the adjectives that modify them to share endings. And so these ancient theoreticians, with one eye on the practical reality of their languages, were reluctant to put them into completely different buckets.

By separating adjectives from substantives in our modern terminology, we've achieved a certain increase in precision on one axis, but at the cost of some significant insight on another. We can more clearly distinguish those two *functions*, and that's useful. We are less able, though, to see how closely nouns and adjectives work together, and that the one can often substitute for the other. If we can appreciate the view from both sides of the fence, we'll be the richer for it.

The other thing that becomes more rigid and more difficult with modern definitions of nouns and adjectives is the place of *pronouns*. The pronoun—Latin *pronomen*, Greek ἀντωνυμία (*antōnymia*)—is one of those (usually) little words that stands in for a noun. Pronouns come in a variety of forms, and we'll talk about them more specifically later. For now, though, it should suffice to note that while pronouns may be more or less inflected than nouns (in English they're more inflected), they tend to stand in for nouns on a one-for-one basis, fulfilling the same function in a sentence or clause. Thus I may say:

He is my friend.

That's more or less the same thing as saying:

Fred is my friend.

The only difference is that it really *means* "Fred is my friend" if and only if we were already talking about Fred in the first place. If we were talking about John, it means that John is my friend. If we were talking about Sally, it will simply break down, because "he" can't refer to Sally.

So the main issue with pronouns is one of *reference*. The difference between a pronoun and any more normal kind of noun (and *functionally* a pronoun *is* a noun) is that, out of context, its meaning is extremely vague, and its reference has to be established *unambiguously* from context. If you've taken many courses that required you to write papers, odds are good that you've at least once (I'm being generous) seen a pronoun circled, and some comment like "Pron. Ref."

in the margin. This is your teacher's way of saying, "Huh? What is this pronoun talking about?" The word or words to which a pronoun refers is usually called its *antecedent*, which is just a fancy Latin way of saying "the word that goes before it." Because the universe is a very odd place, there are occasions where the antecedent comes *after* the pronoun to which it's referring; there are still others where a whole phrase can be the antecedent of a pronoun. This is all somewhat dizzying, I know, but hang in there. We'll talk more about pronouns and how to make sure that they get their required reference later.

For now, though, it's especially important in dealing with nouns and adjectives to note that both Greek and Latin (and English, too, though to a lesser degree) use pronouns to sit athwart the substantive/adjective division. We use the relative pronoun, for example, as a substantive when there's nothing for it to modify, and as an adjective if we want to modify something with it. For example:

> Drake sailed on the *Golden Hind*, **which** was the first English ship
> to go around the world.

Here, "which" is a relative pronoun standing as the subject of its own clause (more about clauses later too—don't fret), referring back to "*Golden Hind*" as its *antecedent*. It's a bit more archaic, but still permissible, to say something like this:

> Drake sailed on the *Golden Hind*, **which** ship was the first English
> craft to go around the world.

"Which" in this case is used *adjectivally*—that is, it functions as an adjective—to modify "ship." Admittedly, "ship" here adds fairly little to the content of the sentence, since we later on specify that it was a craft, but presumably this separates it from the other kinds of craft that might have gone around the world—canoes, hot air balloons, airplanes, and so on.

One can push this to its logical extreme:

> Drake sailed on the *Golden Hind*, **which** English ship was the first
> to go around the world.

This is a little bit chancier, because it leaves open to question whether the *Golden Hind* was the first ship (just happening to be English) to go around the world (as it was not), or whether it was the first *English* ship to go around the world (as it was). In some cases, the ambiguity becomes intolerable; in others it virtually disappears.

Similar to relative pronouns are interrogative pronouns. The interrogative adjectives and pronouns are indistinguishable in form in English, and they're used in questions, with or without nouns more or less as an afterthought. Compare

> Which banana is the ripest?

with

> Which is the ripest?

In the former case, the "which" modifies "banana"; in the second case, it functions as a noun all on its own. Again (and as always with pronouns) we need to be sure that the referent is clear:

> When Tom and Jim finished cleaning out the stables, they wanted
> to split an apple and take a bath, so they asked their mother which
> was ripest.

This relative clause might be understood to be about the apples, or it might be about the way Tom and Jim now smell after their exertions. Clarity of reference is important.

Demonstrative pronouns are another great example of how one word can function both as an adjective and as a substantive. For example,

> Where did you get **that** hat?

Here the demonstrative pronoun (a "pointing-out" pronoun) functions as an adjective, modifying the substantive "hat." On the other hand, it can just as freely be used as a substantive pronoun:

> Where did you get **that**?

Without a noun to modify, the demonstrative pronoun is fully substantive. It will, of course, only refer to a hat if that fact is clear from the context (perhaps the speaker is pointing at the listener's head—and the listener might well respond, if it's unclear, "What, my head? I was born with it"). Without a clear reference, any kind of pronoun is completely useless.

The demonstrative pronouns can be used interchangeably in both substantive and adjective situations in English, Greek, and Latin. When the forms are identical, differentiating between noun (pronoun) and adjective forms becomes a purely academic exercise, driven entirely by context.

The final class of adjectives we should mention are *articles*. English grammar grudgingly considers these to be adjectives, which is why the article is not usually listed as a separate part of speech. We have only three actual articles in English: "the," "a," and "an," of which the last two are variant forms of the same word. We use other words like "some" to fill the role of the article, but they are more properly quantifying adjectives (into which group—see how I used that relative adjective?—we can also put all our numbers as well). These two essential words fall into two categories (they couldn't fall into any more than two)—the *definite* and the *indefinite* article. Calling "the" a definite article merely means that we use "the" to refer to something when what we're talking about is already presumed to be understood; we use the indefinite article "a" or "an" when it's not, and the noun can refer to any eligible referent. Either way, we can apply the article to a noun the way we apply any other adjective—"a house," "gray house." It all seems to work the same way, except that "the" and "a" don't *really* add any descriptive information about the house. Mostly what they tell us is whether its identity is established—either because we've been talking about it before, or because there is a presumption of uniqueness in the referent from the start. As such it's less about the thing itself than about putting it into the context of our discussion up to this point.

Ancient grammarians were not as eager to consider the article an adjective for two reasons, one of them Latin and one of them Greek.

Latin grammarians were not especially interested in classifying articles as adjectives or as anything else because Latin doesn't have an article. The clever ones (the ones who knew Greek as well as Latin) *knew* about articles, but they were happy to dismiss them in their sober Roman way by merely stating that Latin has no article. The Romance languages that grew out of Latin did eventually sprout articles, but these apparently derive from the demonstrative pronoun (which, as we have shown above, can function as a noun or as an adjective), functioning in its adjectival role. Spanish has *el* and *la*, French has *le* and *la*, and so on—all of which are apparently outgrowths of the Latin demonstrative pronoun *ille, illa*.

The Greek reluctance to regard the article as an adjective is somewhat twistier, but just as basic. The Greeks had *lots* of articles—a whole inflected system of them, such that there are twenty-four different ways that the article can take form (though some of those forms are in fact identical). But the Greeks *used* their article rather differently. The Greek article is an athletic little critter. It comes only in a definite form, though it can be made to serve as a kind of demonstrative pronoun. We'll have more to say about this later. There is no indefinite article.

Like its English counterpart "the," the Greek article is used with nouns, and for mostly the same kinds of reasons. (It's not *entirely* identical, though, so its usage needs to be studied and learned.) But it has a very special role, in that it helps, by its position, to define the space in which adjectives of all (other) sorts can be considered to be *attributive*. We'll talk about the difference between attributive and other kinds of adjectives later on, but for now you merely need to know that the space between the article and its noun is a kind of restricted "pocket" into which you can drop adjectives or adjectival phrases to make sure that they modify the noun properly.

The Greek article can also be used with the infinitives of verbs to create an inflected noun (since infinitives really are nouns—we'll talk about these later too) of remarkable subtlety and nuance.

Finally, the Greek article can also be used without nouns altogether, just set apart with a couple of particles, μέν (*men*) and δέ (*de*), to indicate "this one" and "that one."

For all these reasons, Greek theorists regarded their article as something special, and not particularly an adjective.

The one class of adjectives we don't cover above are those that are insolubly confused about their identity: they're verbs as well as adjectives. Those are the participles. The ancient Latin grammarians called this kind of word the *participium*, which is to say, the thing that *takes part* (implicitly, in being both a verb and an adjective, which is to say, an *adjective noun*). The Greeks called it the μετοχή (*metochē*), which means about the same thing—"the with-having thing." They perceived that a participle was a lot like an adjective noun, and a lot like a verb, and they decided that it was important enough to be considered a part of speech on its own. This makes sense, but participles function primarily as supercharged action-oriented adjectives.

We'll have a lot to say about participles later on. What Greek does with the participle is dazzling and brilliant.

## Doing and being

The word "verb" comes more or less directly from Latin *verbum*, which simply means "word." The Greek term is ῥῆμα (*rhēma*).

The verb is the great beating heart of any language. Without at least an implicit verb you can't say anything in any language. Even mathematics (a specialized language, but a language all the same) has its verbs (=, >, and <, among others).

We'll have a lot to say about them later on, but for now it's enough to note that verbs come in two general varieties—*action* verbs and *state-of-being* verbs. Action verbs, as most people readily understand, express some kind of action. They include verbs like these:

|  |  |  |
|---|---|---|
| runs | hit | sings |
| interrogate | begin | circumnavigate |
| wove | taught |  |

Just how active they have to be to qualify as action verbs is open to debate, though even pretty inert "activities" like sitting and lying down come under the heading of "action verbs." The variety of action verbs is enormous, and the ability to identify and use the right one at the right time is one of the hallmarks of a good writer. Energetic prose almost always uses a good range of verbs, while using adjectives and adverbs rather sparingly.

State-of-being verbs are, by contrast, a rather small set. Fortunately or unfortunately, they are also very important. They include obvious verbs of being as well as those that imply coming to be and passing away:

      is                        was                        became
    becomes

One could also reasonably include among state-of-being verbs such borderline cases as

      seems

which is, in some contexts, understood as equivalent to "seems to be."

The state-of-being verb actually is used in two completely different ways, the *copulative* and the *existential*, and it's very important to differentiate between the two, though the form of the verb used itself is typically not any different. We'll discuss this at some length in the next chapter.

Verbs also throw off extra kinds of words that have a verbal origin, but special meanings. These are (usually) what we call *verbals*, which is short for "verbal nouns." They include infinitives, gerunds, and those participles we spoke about so fondly and mysteriously above. We'll talk about which languages have which kinds of verbal nouns later on. Verbal nouns are part of what make these languages interesting, and once you have a handle on how they work, they're not terribly difficult.

## How, when, where, and why

Adverbs answer all kinds of things about the action (or state of being) in a sentence. Later, we'll go into how adverbs and adverbial clauses modify other things, but the adverb is in a very peculiar position in respect to the language: it has the greatest freedom of any word. An adverb, we duly (and perhaps dully) learn, can modify a verb, an adjective, or another adverb. It also sometimes can modify the whole of a sentence—which is really a distinct function, though some would class it as just a special way of modifying the verb.

Seldom do we stop to consider just how shockingly broad this freedom is. The adverb is almost unfettered: it can appear anywhere, with either extraordinary precision or in a way that makes one wonder about the muddiness of the author's thinking. Sometimes it's perfectly obvious:

> He ran **quickly**.

At other times, it can be used with a slovenly disregard for the freedom this gets you:

> He told me to take the book back to the library yesterday.

Did he tell me yesterday that I should at some unspecified time take the book back to the library, or did he tell me at some unpecified time that it was to be returned yesterday?

The adverb also limits the application of an adjective (including the participle):

> **Abruptly** questioning his **unnecessarily** obscure instructions, I offended him.

The adverb can also be daisy-chained to modify another adverb, and so on, though a long string of them becomes hard to follow:

> I **very** soon became tired of waiting.

Here "soon" is an adverb modifying "became tired"; "very" modifies it in turn.

Finally, the adverb modifying a whole sentence is a rare thing, and deserves to be rarer still, but such things do occur. Consider the following:

> **Fortunately**, he has not apparently inherited his father's genetic disease.
> **Hopefully**, he never will.

"Fortunately" in the first of those sentences is construed as what is called a "sentence adverb"—which is to say, it modifies the predication as a whole. It's equivalent to saying, "It is fortunate that . . ." The second sentence, however, represents a usage of "hopefully" that is still frowned on in most grammar books and dictionaries, because (unlike "fortunately") it has a significant meaning as an adverb modifying a verb of human behavior. For example,

> "Is there any cake left?" he asked **hopefully**.

It's not the case that the speaker of the sentence is hoping that the subject asked this: rather, the sentence is saying that the subject asked about the cake *in a hopeful manner.* Most grammarians and lexical hard-liners continue to consider this the only legitimate sense of "hopefully." In the previous instance, that meaning is confounded with the broader (but increasingly common) usage. After all, it's rather ludicrous to talk about inheriting a disease in a hopeful manner. Complicating life for the hard-liners, though, is the fact that the misuse of "hopefully" has a very long history, despite its ambiguities, and it corresponds to the German adverb *hoffentlich*, which really *is* a sentence adverb—meaning precisely what purists believe that English "hopefully" does not.

All in all, the adverbial *function*—both as a part of speech and as a category of clause—is among the most interesting and challenging any language has to offer. We use adverbial constructions of various sorts in a thousand different ways to shape context for the meanings of our sentences. The backbone of any sentence is about "who" and "what"—the subject and the predicate. Adverbs and adverbial clauses answer all the rest: "when," "where," "why," "how," and so on. By limiting the scope of absolute predication the humble adverb allows us to live in the day-to-day world.

Ancient grammarians also understood the preposition as a distinct kind of word, but they recognized what modern language historians also recognize—that it's a direct descendant of the adverb, and even today it has not completely broken free of its roots. In the sentence

I'm going out.

the adverb "out" is simple. It answers the question *where* for the simple verb "going." But the same word can seamlessly slide into the role of a preposition when it's set up before an object:

I'm going out the door.

One can similarly use some other prepositions the same way: "in," "by," and a number of others are dual-purpose words, and most dictionaries will gloss them as being prepositions and adverbs. This is not because they exhibit two distinct functions, but because prepositions really are fossilized adverbs, frozen in place with respect to a noun or pronoun that comes to be seen as an object.

Some English prepositions no longer retain this ambiguity of function. One can't simply say, in normal modern English:

I'm going into.

or

She ran from.

Be that as it may, all prepositions in English, the Germanic languages generally, and Latin and Greek come *originally* from some kind of adverbial formulation, and the marks of that kinship are never entirely erased. In the early histories of all these languages the distinction is particularly shaky, such that in Homeric Greek (as in Old High German or Old English), virtually any preposition can be used without an object as a simple adverb.

## Language glue

There are some words that really don't have any meaning in and of themselves—not even the vague kind of meaning we get from a pronoun without a reference. They don't refer to persons, places, or things; they don't refer to actions; they don't even refer to how actions happen to or on account of persons, places, or things. These are words like "and," "but," and so on. English recognizes them as *conjunctions*. In Latin a conjunction is unsurprisingly called a *coniunctio*, and in Greek a σύνδεσμος (*syndesmos*), both of which mean something like a "tying-together" or "fastening." It binds things together, and establishes the relationship between one word, clause, or phrase and another.

Conjunctions come under the broader class that late Latin grammarians (specifically Priscian, following Aristotle) referred to as the *syncategoremata*. There's no particular reason you need to know that word now, but it really sounds rather elegant, doesn't it? Seven-syllable words are not that common.

## Herbs and spices

When I was living off campus one summer at college, my housemates and I were making omelets for dinner one evening. We had a variety of ingredients for the omelet: some onions, some cheese, and a few kinds of herbs. I was gleefully composing an omelet for myself when I took the jar of oregano from the shelf and gave it a good shake.

I was sure there was a shaker top on that jar. But there wasn't. As a result, about a tablespoon of oregano went into my congealing egg mixture. We were living on a spare budget, so, rather than waste it, I ate it. But I couldn't stand the taste of oregano for some years afterward.

Interjections are like that. They are unnecessary from an informational standpoint, just as herbs and spices are generally nutritionally unnecessary. They fill no real semantic or syntactic function, but add flavors—for good or ill, depending on how they're handled. A good writer, like a good chef, can use a few such words to brilliant effect. But more is not necessarily better: even the good ones turn nasty if they're overused. Too often one finds prose in which no sentence is allowed to pass without some extra attitudinal marker. The result quickly becomes cloying.

The category of interjections covers a wide variety of savory and unsavory terms, but the feature they share is that they are syntactically absolute—that is, they're unconnected, not tied in to anything else in the sentence or clause. They include things like "Lo!" and "Oh!," as well as other expletives (another word for an interjection) that are best deleted (or better yet, never uttered at all).

Because interjections weren't organic to the structure of a clause, Greek and Latin grammarians tended not to classify them as parts of speech at all. Obviously they *are* parts of speech, since people speak them (in part), but the concern of the ancient grammarians was more for the logical cohesion of the sentence than for accounting for all possible noises people might make along the way.

More intriguing, and generally more meaningful, is the category of words the Greeks knew as the particles. This is the last part of speech we'll be talking about. From our point of view, most of the particles could probably be classified as adverbs or conjunctions, since they either supply something to the sentence that indicates the speaker's attitude toward it, or they relate parts to each other. They are little words like μέν and δέ (*men* and *de*: markers of balance, sometimes overtranslated as "on the one hand . . . on the other"), γάρ (*gar*: the inferential sense of "for"), and the amazing ἄν (*an*), which has never been translated at all, but which has a profound influence on every sentence and clause it touches, and can at a stroke make what is real in the past into something that is hypothetical in the present, or what is only wishful into something that is a possibility. A whole book (imaginatively entitled *The Greek Particles*) has been written on the subject by J. D. Denniston. This may sound like as dull a work as can be conceived, but you'll know you've arrived at the acute stages of grammatical geekdom when you actually enjoy reading it. It's fascinating.

# CHAPTER 2

# The Parts of a Sentence

*How it's all a lot simpler than it seems, and why the technical
vocabulary really describes how it works*

In talking about the parts of a sentence, we move to a more philosophical and abstract level. At bottom, however, it's shockingly simple. It's been obscured with some archaic vocabulary that students often find intimidating, but it makes perfectly good sense when you understand what it refers to.

## The two main parts

Here's the simple fact about speaking (or writing). The function of every sentence, always, is to *say* something *about* something. That's all. Every sentence, whether statement, question, or command, does that. Accordingly every sentence has two fundamental parts—the what-it's-about part, which is traditionally called the *subject*, and the what-about-it part, which is traditionally called the *predicate*. What's more, that's *all* any sentence has—there's nothing in a sentence that's *not* part of one or the other.

As simple as it is, it's an enormously important theoretical truth to grasp—the fundamental fact about how all languages work. You *have* to be talking about something; you *have* to be saying something about it. The subject is what the sentence is about, and the predicate is what you are saying about it. This may sound rather plodding and maybe a little too simple—but it's just about the only definition that really holds water in the long term.

Some modern linguists have distinguished these two parts as "NP" and "VP," standing for "noun part" and "verb part," but, although this is a convenient shorthand, it is not really as accurate as the old terminology. It's true that the predicate is the part of the sentence normally associated with the verb—but that's because saying something about something *usually* requires a verb or its equivalent. It is not, however, *absolutely* required in all cases. Almost any student of elementary

Greek will have encountered this sentence:

ἀγαθὸς ὁ ἄνθρωπος.

This is a complete, legitimate sentence, yet it has no verb. Literally and narrowly, it can be translated as "Good the person," but in terms of idiomatic meaning, it is the normal way of saying, "The person is good." None of its three words is a verb.

Latin does the same thing, almost as frequently. So, in fact, does English, though usually it takes the form of an exclamation:

Happy the man who knows his friends.

We may mentally supply "is," but this is considered a reasonably good sentence without it, even in English. Hence the "associated with the verb" definition of a predicate is at best shaky. What we can consider pretty much absolute is the "what you're saying about the subject" definition. In philosophical terms, saying something about anything is called *predication*. We say that we are predicating something *of* something else.

## Predication

The notion of predication is important for a number of reasons—one being that the logic of this system of language is consistent with a larger philosophical system. Aristotle in his logical works spends a great deal of energy outlining the problem of predication, and those works (known collectively as the Organon, containing the *Categories, On Interpretation*, the *Prior Analytics*, the *Posterior Analytics*, and the *Sophistical Refutations*) remain the foundation of most subsequent logical thought down to the late nineteenth century. The title of the first of his logical works, now generally called the *Categories*, might perhaps more accurately be translated as *Predicates*. It really is nothing more or less than a discussion of what you can say about any subject. In Aristotle's metaphysically rooted grammar, the subject is called the *hypokeimenon* (ὑποκείμενον), which denotes the "underlying" or "having-been-placed-under [thing]," from ὑπό (under) and κεῖμαι (lie), which is more or less what *subiectum* (from *sub*, "under," and *iacio*, "throw, place") means as well.

A predicate, on the other hand, is a *katēgoria* (κατηγορία)—a compound of κατά (according to) and ἀγορεύω (speak)—from which, similarly, Latin *praedicatum* is drawn (from *prae*, "before" [and in some contexts, "about"], and *dicatum*, "[thing] said"). The word κατηγορία (sometimes κατηγόρημα) originally meant "accusation" in legal language, and there is some obvious parallelism here: what is brought as an accusation against a defendant in a trial is precisely what is being *said* of him.

The remarkable symmetry of Aristotle's system can be seen in his use of the same terminology in his metaphysics: matter (in its primary and undifferentiated form) is also the *hypokeimenon*—that which receives form or predicates when it is part of something particular. It would be too circuitous to go into all those implications here, but it is important to understand that the idea of predication, as something that happens to a subject, runs very deep, and its consequences have been worked out fairly well. Any predicate noun or predicate adjective can form a predicate, though often it's accompanied by a verb of being; any action verb can form a predicate as well.

Predication, therefore, is merely the action of attaching a predicate to a subject—in other words, saying something about something. This is what happens in every meaningful sentence, and it's all that happens, strictly.

The hidden catch is that while every sentence contains or is made up of a predication, not *every* predication constitutes a sentence: some are merely *parts* of sentences. Whether it turns out to be a whole sentence or just a part, however, *any* complete predication is called a *clause*. Only a complete predication—a combination, in other words, of a subject and a predicate—can be considered a clause. Sentences are made up of one or more clauses.

## Two kinds of predication

In both practical and theoretical terms, this business of predication can be broken down into two basic types. We can predicate certain *properties* or *characteristics* of things, or we can predicate *actions* of them. The first type is probably the simpler to understand, though it is less common in ordinary discourse:

> My house is blue.
> My house is in Bavaria.
> The distance around the world is about 25,000 miles.

This is the simplest form of predication (though there are some nasty shoals lurking not far beneath the surface). Most such predication takes the form of a sentence using the verb "is," or something like it. In many languages and in many situations, even that verb can be omitted. Other verbs that function similarly will do the same job ("becomes," "seems," and so forth, in English). Mostly what the verb of being does in such situations is to connect a subject ("my house," "the distance") with something that it *is*. The predicate is typically dominated by a noun or an adjective. There's some debate about whether we should even consider the verb "is" a philosophically meaningful part of the predicate. We'll get back to that later. For the time being, however, it's worth noting chiefly that this is not very useful for describing what's going on. There's no option here for going fishing or conquering Gaul or eating dinner. It's an extremely *useful* category of predication for putting things in order, but if it were all we had, it would be an extremely static and stale world.

We'll talk a lot more about predicating action when we come to verbs. For now, however, we'll merely note that predicates virtually always require a verb.

## Two kinds of being

This discussion opens up a question that stands on the border between grammar and philosophy. It's of enormous importance, and yet it's an unresolved—and possibly unresolvable—issue.

It stems from the fact that the verb of being is used in two very different ways. Most people who aren't actually wrestling with the philosophical implications, however, usually don't have to differentiate between these two uses, at least not consciously.

The most common use of the state-of-being verb is as what we call the *copula*, which means something like "the fastener." When I'm saying that a house is blue, I'm attaching the adjective descriptor "blue" to the subject "house"—and that's all. It's important to realize that this attachment *entails no actual assertion that the subject actually exists*. Consider the following three sentences:

> My house **is** blue.
> My house **is** in Bavaria.
> A unicorn **is** a one-horned creature.

All three of these are equally valid uses of the copula. My house really *does* exist, and it really *is* blue, but the fact that it *exists* has nothing to do with what the sentence is stating. The sentence is entirely about its color.

The second sentence may actually help explain this somewhat better, by factoring out the irrelevant. My house still really exists, and it's still blue, but it's nowhere near Bavaria. The fact that it is not in Bavaria means that the sentence is *false*, but that fact doesn't really have anything to say about the *existence* of the house as such, either.

The third sentence should drive the point home, though some will have trouble with it. Here the verb of being is both a valid use of the copula *and true*, though this is still not because unicorns exist (to the best of my knowledge, they do not exist, and never have). But it's true as a definitional statement about the term "unicorn": the *definition* of a unicorn is that it is a one-horned creature. If I were to see such a creature, it is on the basis of this definition that I would recognize it as a unicorn. Thus *as a copula*, this is a perfectly legitimate use of the word "is." It's still not a statement of existence, though.

In Greek and Latin, and sometimes in English, we can have an *implied* copula. In Greek, you can say this:

> ἀγαθὸς ὁ ἄνθρωπος.
>
> *Good the person.*
>
> *(I.e., The person [is] good.)*

In English:

> Happy the man whose wish and care
> a few paternal acres bound,
> content to breathe his native air
> in his own ground.
>
> —Alexander Pope, "Ode on Solitude"

Neither of those makes the actual verb of being explicit in the sentence. In English, it sounds awfully high-flown, but it's accepted. In Greek, it's the normal way of forming a copula. In Latin, it happens fairly frequently. Note again that none of this says anything about the existence of such good people or happy men, whether there is one or millions of them—or none at all. It's joining the predicate "happy" to the subject "the man . . . ."

The other use of the state-of-being verb is radically different—it's the one that *does* assert existence, and we call it, on that account, the *existential* use of the verb of being. This has nothing to do with the philosophical school known as existentialism, aside from the fact that both claim to have something to do with being. We have fairly restricted ways in almost any language to assert the existence of something. In English we use a supplementary "there" (a word normally cited in dictionaries as an adverb, though in this context arguably more of a particle). "There are unicorns" would be an actual positive claim of their existence.

The existential verb of being is clearly important: when it's necessary to do at all, asserting the existence of something is probably the most important thing one can say about it. But it's much less *common* than the uses of the verb of being as a copula.

As noted, in English, we tend to use a meaningless placeholder adverb, "there," when we want to use an existential verb of being. We say:

> **There is** a delightful campground on Mount Rainier.

or

> **There are** two uses for the state-of-being verb.

This nonlocating "there" can even extend to other verbs that are not normally considered state-of-being verbs:

> In a hole in the ground **there lived** a hobbit.
> —J. R. R. Tolkien, *The Hobbit*

In Latin, the same word—*est* or *sunt*—is used for both situations, but the existential *est* is often distinguished from the copulative usage by its position in the sentence. Latin authors will most often push the *est* or *sunt* right up to the front of the sentence. As such, it's the whole predicate, and the rest of the sentence lives in a relative clause attached to the implicit subject, just to make it completely obvious that the *sunt* is *not* just being used to tie the subject to another predicate:

> Sunt qui . . .
> *[There] are [those] who . . .*

Greek can do something similar. If you've done much Latin, you have probably encountered this construction. It tends to have a sense much akin to "Some people . . . ," and there it's right on the edge of making an existential assertion. How you take it will depend on context.

In Latin or Greek, there is no equivalent "flagging" word like "there." Existential uses of state-of-being verbs are *not* left to be supplied by the reader as copulative state-of-being verbs often are.

This becomes a philosophical problem when we confront the question of whether asserting the existence of something is actually a *predicate* in any legitimate sense at all. Can existence *be* predicated in the same way as we can predicate goodness or blueness of a subject? Philosophical conundrums swirl around the category, and it's harder to nail down than one might expect.

## Two kinds of clause

Grammarians love to classify things, and they've been at it for well over two thousand years, so a certain amount of conventional terminology has arisen to describe how sentences go together. Some of them are probably obvious to you, but just to be thorough, we'll go through them. You will discover that knowing them is really not very hard, and it's more trouble than it's worth to ignore them.

The first and most important distinction that arises here is between those clauses that can stand on their own as a complete sentence and those that can't.

Clauses that can stand out there all by themselves as complete sentences are known as *independent* clauses. That is, they don't depend on anything else for their existence, and they don't require any other clauses to give them meaning. Most of those things we've been citing as simple examples above belong to this group:

> I went to the store.
> Thomas hit the baseball with his tennis racket.

These examples seem fairly obvious. It needs to be pointed out that the distinction between dependent and independent clauses is not based on whether you need context to make *sense* out of them. Some sentences convey almost no information without some other sentences around them. Consider these sentences:

> He did so.
> We didn't agree with that.
> I forbid it.

You really have no idea what any of these means in terms of *substance*—but as sentences, they are free of all other encumbrances.

The other kind of clause is the *dependent* clause, sometimes also called the *subordinate* clause. It's fairly easy to figure out what "dependent" means, but "subordinate" is perhaps a little trickier. It merely means "[that which is] arranged under" (from Latin *sub*, "under," and *ordinare*, "to arrange, position"). "Subordinate" reflects the usage of those grammatically clever Greeks, who called such clauses *hypotactic*, a term that comes from ὑπό (*hypo*, "under") and τάττω (*tattō*, "arrange") or τάξις (*taxis*, "arrangement"). Subordinate clauses don't merely fail to express complete ideas; we also can't really conceive of them as standing alone as sentences. They are clauses like these:

> When the sun goes down . . .
> Whether you like goat cheese or not . . .
> . . . who told me the story
> . . . that it was not the same person

Note that these are not just random selections of words, or any selected phrase. They all *are* indeed distinct and complete clauses. Each one has a subject ("the sun," "you," "who," "it") and a predicate ("goes down," "like goat cheese or not," "told me the story," and "was not the same person"). There are other kinds of phrases that don't have both subject and predicate, and these we will deal with later. For now we just need to worry about clauses.

The other thing to know about subordinate clauses in general is that each one depends in a precisely defined way on one other clause. The clause it depends on can be either a simple sentence or may itself be a subordinate clause that depends on something else—with the result that clauses can take the shape of a kind of "tree" of dependency. Remember this: it's important.

## Three kinds of independent clause

An independent clause can really have three functions—and those are, effectively, the functions of the sentence it controls, even if there are other kinds of clauses attached to the independent clause.

First, and most common, an independent clause can make a statement. We've seen plenty of these already:

> Caesar conquered Gaul.

Second, it can ask a question:

> Is that fish fresh?

Third, it can give a command:

> Take your hat.

Any and every sentence will do one of these three things; which one it does will depend on what the main clause—the top-level independent clause—of the sentence is doing. All other clauses in a sentence exist only to serve the main clause. Grammar is not very democratic.

## Three kinds of sentence

Now that we have the two kinds of clause in hand, we can go further and classify sentences as combinations of those kinds. In fact this classification is really not nearly as important as the previous one, since if you don't know it, you can still get along based on what you *do* know: but it's worth bearing in mind, since you will run into the terms fairly frequently in a variety of places, and it makes it a little easier to talk about grammatical structures.

The first and simplest kind of sentence is, unsurprisingly, called the *simple sentence*. It contains one clause, and one only. This must by definition be an independent clause. That is, it has a subject and a predicate, and it does not depend on any other clause for its fundamental meaning. As a whole, it performs one of the three functions of a sentence; it makes a statement, asks a question, or gives a command:

> Caesar conquered Gaul.
> Is that fish fresh?
> Take your hat.

> The man in the back of the store with the cat and the big red nose
> gave me a box of potatoes just beginning to sprout.

Even in a simple sentence, a subject or a predicate can be compound—that is, made up of more than one part. There is still only one predication in place. Compound subjects or predicates can be short or long, but they tend not to be exceedingly long:

> Caesar conquered Gaul and invaded Britain.
> Are those fish and these apples fresh?
> Take your hat and go.

As soon as one stitches two or more independent clauses together with a conjunction like "but" or "and," however, the result is what we call a *compound sentence*:

> Caesar conquered Gaul, but Alexander conquered Persia.
> Eat your dinner of fresh fish, and then take your hat and go.

Compound sentences are of course typically longer than simple sentences, but they are not much more difficult to understand. The only thing that distinguishes them from simple sentences is that they contain at least two predications. One needs to remember which parts go with which.

The third kind of sentence is really the interesting one: it's called a *complex sentence*, and it's any sentence that has *at least one subordinate clause*. Complex sentences can have one independent clause or more; if so, we sometimes talk about them as compound complex sentences, but those get relatively little special attention as a separate class. Dependent clauses are so arranged that they can be joined to main clauses, or made dependent on subordinate clauses themselves. They can become very long and potentially very complex, but they need not be. Here are a few complex sentences:

> If we die, we die.

> Although Caesar was the first to conquer Gaul, Alexander had earlier conquered Persia and parts of India.

> Are those fish that you brought home yesterday still fresh?

> When, in the course of human events, it becomes necessary for one people to dissolve the political bonds which have connected them with another, and to assume among the powers of the earth, the separate and equal station to which the laws of nature and of nature's God entitle them, a decent respect to the opinions of mankind requires that they should declare the causes which impel them to the separation.
>
> —Thomas Jefferson, *Declaration of Independence*

> Although I am afraid, O judges, that it is a base thing for one who is beginning to speak for a very brave man to be alarmed, and though it is far from becoming, when Titus Annius Milo himself is more disturbed for the safety of the republic than for his own, that I should not be able to bring to the cause a similar greatness of mind, yet this novel appearance of a new manner of trial alarms my eyes, which, wherever they fall, seek for the former customs of the forum and the ancient practice in trials.
>
> —Cicero, *In Defense of Milo*; trans. C. D. Yonge

We can even sometimes have sentences in which the dependency forms a kind of "daisy chain" of connection. Seldom is the result very pretty, but we can understand it well enough:

> This is the cow with the crumpled horn that tossed the dog that worried the cat that killed the rat that ate the malt that lay in the house that Jack built.
>
> —Traditional

The more complex parts of grammatical study derive from the construction and arrangement of these subordinate clauses, therefore, and they tend to be far more varied in type and internal makeup than independent clauses. They are, however, still relatively manageable if one just breaks them down into types.

# Three kinds of subordinate clause

This is where chapters 1 and 2 come together. The trick in controlling subordinate clauses is really fairly trivial, but most people don't know it all the same: it is in realizing that any sentence, no matter how complex, is effectively a permutation or elaboration of the simple sentence, and that *every subordinate clause that appears in a complex sentence fulfills the function of some simpler part of speech in the clause on which it depends.* There are exactly three kinds of such clauses, each taking on the role of a specific part of speech. One kind acts as an adverb, and these are typically called adverbial clauses. One acts as a (substantive) noun, and these are typically called noun clauses (or sometimes, in stodgier old grammars, substantive clauses or object clauses). The last kind acts as an adjective. Because the world is a twisty and unpredictable place, these are seldom called adjectival clauses, though the term is in use. They're usually called *relative* clauses, but there are actually some kinds of relative clauses that are functionally adverbial, so keep the "adjectival" designation at least somewhere in the back of your mind. It will save you grief later.

The next chapter is largely devoted to elaborating each of these three kinds of clause. For now, we'll just offer a few examples to show how they function as parts of speech. Here's a sentence using a noun clause as its subject:

> That he went behind my back troubles me.

The main (independent) clause here is "_____ troubles me." Normally we would put a noun (with any relevant modifiers) in the blank space:

> **The weather** troubles me.
> *Your belligerent attitude* troubles me.
>
> *This impudent, self-righteous rascal with the obnoxious attitude* troubles me.

Those are simple sentences—even the long one at the end. Whatever we put into the blank is the *subject* of the sentence, therefore—it's what we're talking about. Normally, that is a function taken up by a noun. The predicate—what we're saying about the subject—is "troubles me." So it is here also. "That he went behind my back" functions *exactly* as a noun does in the place of the subject. When we use a clause rather than some other simpler sort of noun (substantive), we wind up with a complex sentence, but in all other ways the function is identical.

Here's an adverbial clause in action:

**When I was a little boy,** the clown sang about the rain.

Here we have a complete sentence, with a subject and a predicate: "the clown" is what the sentence is about, and hence the subject. What we're saying *about* the clown is that he sang about the rain. The bold portion is functioning here as an adverb—that is, telling us (in this case) *when* the clown was singing. It could also be used to tell us where or in what manner or any of those other things one can do with an adverb. Here are other adverbs or adverbial phrases in the same position:

Saturday the clown sang about the rain.
Softly the clown sang about the rain.
In Shakespeare's play the clown sang about the rain.

There are many kinds of adverbial clauses. We'll talk about them in the next chapter.

Finally, here's an adjectival clause in action. It's a little less obviously identical to an adjective in the sentence, because we normally put simple adjectives in *front* of the nouns they're modifying (at least in English), whereas we usually put adjectival clauses after their nouns, but their *function* is the same:

I killed the rat **that ate the malt.**

Here again, the adjectival clause plays a secondary role in the sentence—that is, it's neither the central subject ("I") nor the main predicate ("killed the rat"). It *is*, however, modifying "the rat." It's telling us *what* rat we're talking about. I killed the rat *that ate the malt*, but not the one that ate the bacon, or the giant rat of Sumatra. If we were to use simple adjectives, as noted, they would normally precede "rat" in English, but that's primarily an accident of English (it's different in Latin, though not generally in Greek):

I killed the black rat.
I killed the huge rat.
I killed the huge black rat.

If we use anything other than a simple adjective, though, the phrase will tend to follow the word it's modifying, rather than preceding it:

I killed the rat from the backyard.
I killed the rat of Sumatra.

One can even combine them:

> I killed the giant rat of Sumatra.

The placement of these phrases and words does not change the fact that all of them are adjectival in function. In a language with a higher tolerance than English has for embedded adjectival phrases, one could say: "I killed the giant of-Sumatra rat." English speakers wouldn't normally do this, but Greek would be perfectly at home with it. On the same principle, one could say: "I killed the that-ate-the-malt rat" or " . . . the having-eaten-the-malt rat." Again, we normally *wouldn't* do so, but most hearers would probably understand the sentence. It's hard to come up with a categorical reason proving that this is ungrammatical, but it is at least so unidiomatic that most native speakers would take some time sorting it out, and would never produce such a sentence.

## Phrases that aren't clauses

As we have already emphasized, a clause is a formally defined piece of a sentence that contains a subject and a predicate of its own. Every clause has a subject, and every clause has a predicate. There are *other* combinations of words that function organically in a sentence, without a subject and a predicate. We call these by the looser name *phrases*, and the category includes all manner of combinations of words, including prepositional phrases, which function as extended adjectives or adverbs:

> The car **in the garage** is not in good order.
> He was running **along the beach**.

We will have occasion to discuss these somewhat more later on, when we're looking at the various cases of nouns, and how they are deployed.

# CHAPTER 3

# Adverbial Clauses—Every Which Way

*A survey of adverbial clauses, and how they form*
*clusters of meaning*

As explained in the previous chapter, subordinate clauses fall into three broad categories, according to how they operate in a sentence. They can operate as adverbs, adjectives, or nouns. By far the most common are the adverbial clauses, which is what we'll be talking about in this chapter.

There are a few kinds of noun clauses, and really only one main kind of adjectival clause. By contrast, there seem to be a plethora of adverbial clauses. In fact there are not *that* many. Nine categories will encompass most if not all of them, and they can be further clustered into a few more basic groups.

There are simple adverbial clauses that describe attendant circumstances, such as *where* something happens, or *how* it happens. There are adverbial clauses that have to do with *why* something happens—purposes, causes, and so on. There are adverbial clauses that detail *to what effect* something happens—results. These are a lot like purpose clauses, but need to be kept at least somewhat distinct. Finally, there are adverbial clauses that have to do with the complexities of time and contingency—*when* or *if* something happens. These are the most complicated, so we'll leave them for last.

## An overview of adverbial clauses

While some grammarians tend to dismiss the various categories of adverbial clauses with a wave of the hand, as if there were altogether too many different kinds to mention, in fact there aren't very many kinds of things you can explore with an adverb at the most fundamental level, and hence there aren't many kinds of things you can say with an adverbial clause.

We can produce a rough categorization of adverbial clauses by resorting to the journalist's short list of questions that should ideally be addressed in any news article: *who, what, when, where, how, why.* To these we may add the equally important question, *so what.*

The "who" and "what" part of a sentence are already taken care of by the subject and the verb. They are the main matter—they tell who (or what) is doing (or being) what. The rest of the categories, however, fall squarely within the domain of the adverb. As we discussed in chapter 1, adverbs give shape and color to a sentence, and, more importantly, often limit the scope of predication. In some languages, these complex adverbial modifications are handled by clauses; in others, some of them are handled using other not-quite-clausal structures (for example, in Attic Greek, a "clause" of proviso or of natural result is actually an expression involving an infinitive verb: this prevents it from strictly being a clause, but it's convenient to treat it as one in most situations). Let's break these uses down by category.

## Cause and effect

Many of the adverbs (and hence adverbial clauses) we employ on a daily basis are concerned with the problem of cause and effect, and with the mental processes that *link* cause and effect—namely, those involving intention or inference. Together they make up a knotty and somewhat problematic mass of adverbial clauses that are easily distinguished in theory, but may be harder to separate in practice.

Probably the first sort of adverbial clause you will have learned, if you have studied any Latin or Greek, is either the purpose clause or the result clause. These are fairly similar in construction in both English and Latin. Greek makes some important distinctions that add a little bit of subtlety to the picture.

The difference between a purpose clause and a result clause is easy to comprehend, but sometimes it's difficult to tell which kind you're looking at: it's at this point that context becomes critical. The two kinds of clause really answer two different questions: *why* and *so what.*

### Why?

Causal clauses are probably the simplest to understand and to construct. The simplicity is, however, illusory. In fact, the notion of causation is a profound and difficult one philosophically: while all people—and even most higher animals—seem to have hardwired some notion of causation (at least one reason to consider it an important category of thought), there are few if any ways in which causation can be established purely deductively. It is always inferred from observation—usually repeated observation of sequential phenomena—and though science has come up with a number of ways to try to differentiate coincidental sequences of events from the truly causal, the assumption is at best tentative, even for those things that seem obvious to us. Causality is sufficiently problematic in formal logic that mistaken inferences have earned their own name as a logical fallacy: *post hoc, ergo propter hoc,* "after this, therefore because of this."

In terms of language, however, we need not be overly concerned with this conundrum: the use of a causal clause implies (at least) the speaker's assertion that the one thing led to another. It may also represent the general sense of a wider community (embracing, usually, the hearer as well as the speaker) about that relationship. Whether true causality can ever be tested objectively is a separate problem, but not primarily a problem of language as such.

An assertion of causation remains a large and philosophically based claim, however. It is most importantly distinguished from *purpose* and *result*—which we'll talk about next.

### To what purpose?

A purpose clause represents not the direct reason something occurred, but the *desired effect* in the mind of the agent, which is significantly different. For example,

Tom emptied the pail on the fire **in order to put it out**.

That was his intention. The result may have been different, as we can see from the following causal clarification:

**Because the pail held gasoline,** it merely made the fire worse.

The latter tells us the actual cause of the actual result, not Tom's intention in doing what he did, or anything about the manner in which he did it. But the reason for doing something is important—and people's motivations are central to everything we have to say about them, in stories and songs and the daily news.

This brings us, therefore, to the second sense of the word "why"—*why* (with what intended end in view) did someone *do* what he or she did? That is, what were the reasons of the thinking agent? Consider these examples:

Tom emptied the bucket in order to put out the fire.

Cicero cleverly used his hearers' knowledge of the form of Roman oration **[in order] to mislead them.**

In English, "in order" is not essential for the formation of a purpose clause, but it is often used to distinguish the purpose clause from other similar clauses where the phrasing might lead to ambiguity. When in doubt, it's probably a good idea to use it, unless the context is already getting too wordy.

Again, note that because the purpose clause expresses the *reason* somebody does something, and reports on the agent's *intention*, only a sentient agent can have a purpose clause attributed to him or her. We cannot normally say, unless we are personifying trees:

> The tree fell over in order to crush the house.

This would be to attribute intention to trees, which, as far as we know, do not formulate plans or ideas. We *can*, however, say:

> The tree was pushed over in order to crush the house.

The subject of this sentence is still "the tree." It is no more capable of forming a plan than the previous tree was, but the purpose clause quietly attaches itself to the presumed agent—whoever or whatever was doing the pushing. Or we can say:

> The bulldozer operator knocked over the tree in order to crush the house.

We can also say:

> The giant stomped heavily in order to crush the house.

## So what?

*Result clauses* straddle these distinctions. A result clause can be seen as a kind of causal clause viewed from the opposite side of the problem. In its purest form, it simply expresses the *consequence* of some action, whether it expressed any intention or not:

> The tree fell over so that the house was crushed.
> The giant stomped heavily so that the house was crushed.
> The bulldozer operator rammed the tree so that it fell over.

None of these examples expresses the *intention* of the tree (normally thought to be incapable of intention), the giant (who might be causing this mayhem either intentionally or inadvertently), or the bulldozer operator (probably intentionally). It could well have been the case that the giant was pursuing a program of demolition; it is equally likely (from a linguistic point of view) that he was merely incompetent. We might assume, given the right context, that he was a friendly giant, and had the best of intentions, hoping to spare all the structures in his path, but that, being clumsy, he failed.

Greek formally distinguishes between the natural result of an action and its actual result. English can also distinguish between these things, but does so with accompanying words, rather than through the clause's structure. The difference between the two kinds of result can be seen in the following pair of sentences:

> The tree fell over so as to crush the house.
> The tree fell over so that the house was crushed.

These may seem nearly identical; but one could follow the first (but not the second) sentence with an explanation of how it failed to come about:

> The tree fell over so as to crush the house, but the friendly giant
> caught it in time and tossed it harmlessly aside.

The distinction between actual result and purpose is fairly easy to grasp: the *natural* result construction, however, stands somewhere between the two, and indeed often weakly suggests purpose:

> Hubert drove so as to cause accidents wherever he went.

This isn't actually saying that he set out to cause accidents, but it does seem to imply that he didn't take adequate precautions to prevent them. Natural result arguably is more concerned with the question *how* than with the *why* we associate with the purpose clause or the *so what* of the actual result clause.

The Greek natural result construction is not strictly a clause at all, since it uses an infinitive verb (thus violating the stricture that the predicate of a true clause must contain a *finite* verb), but it behaves in most other ways like a clause, and most of the English and Latin ways of phrasing this *will* qualify as clauses. In English we can say, "so as to . . . ," which uses the infinitive (and hence is not a clause either), or "so that it might . . . ," which uses a finite verb (and so is a clause). In Latin the subjunctive form dominates; infinitive pseudoclauses are rare, and can probably be attributed to a deliberate Hellenizing impulse.


## When and if: Time and contingency

Two problematic philosophical concepts—time and contingency—converge here. They intersect in ways we probably don't fully understand, but the human mind has nevertheless been able to formulate a number of useful sentences that depend on different senses of time and contingency.

Time is one of the most elusive and evocative concepts we have. The passage of time is impossible to measure objectively from any standpoint outside time, and we experience it subjectively. It challenges poets, philosophers, and physicists; it also challenges grammarians.

Time has enormous bearing on the nature of predication. The operation of any verb depends on the twin properties of *tense* and *aspect*. "Tense" refers chiefly to the place of anything in time; "aspect" to how we are considering the "shape" of the action, or its relation to the speaker. Though we may not know exactly what time means or how it works, we clearly have some very complex ideas about it, and they give rise to a vast range of ways of talking about the relationships between different events in time. Much of this we'll take up when we look at the verb and the ideas of tense and aspect in particular. For now, we'll confine ourselves to how adverbial clauses deal with time.

One of the things that's peculiar about time (at least from our perspective) is that it's not symmetrical. The past is almost infinitely different from the future, precisely because while the past is absolutely unchangeable, the future is not. In philosophical terms, we talk about the one being *determinate* and the other *indeterminate*. Some believe that the future is just as determined as the past, but nobody has been able to prove the case one way or the other: in either case, it probably has almost nothing to do with how we *perceive* the future. Whether future events are intrinsically indeterminate or whether our sense of indeterminacy merely reflects the incompleteness of our knowledge, we can speak only from that perspective.

Accordingly we talk about the future as being *contingent*—that is, subject to some degree of chance or intentional alteration. We may of course be reasonably certain, even before it happens, that the water glass we drop out a third-story window onto the pavement below is going to break. That's a reasonable effect to project from the cause—but until it happens, it is still to some degree contingent. What has not yet happened is fundamentally different in kind from what *has* happened; the present is the infinitely thin boundary that separates the one kind of reality from the other. To say that something is contingent is also to say that it depends on something, though we may not know what. Thus it is woven up with all the "ifs" that surround our lives as well. The concept of "if" is tied up with our concept of time: consider the fact that the temporal adverb "then" is often used to follow it inferentially:

If you break the glass, then you will have to pay for it.
If a number is divisible by six, then it is not prime.

## Doing or keeping time

The clauses that answer the question *when* we call *temporal.* That is, they're about *time* (from Latin *tempus, temporis,* "time"). But it should come as no surprise that they really fall into two fundamentally different classes—those relating to the present or past, and those relating to the future. These behave differently, and they are constructed differently, largely because they are operating with a very different sense of time. One is determinate, and the other is seen as contingent.

Another theoretical axis runs through temporal clauses, too: we often need to distinguish between the *general* and the *particular.* Statements about the past may refer to single incidents, or they may refer to a pattern of occurrence. While there may be no formal distinction separating them in English, the meaning is nevertheless quite different, depending on context. Consider the following examples; only the first sentence has changed:

> Aunt Matilda visited us only once that I can recall. When she came, we had a huge party, with dozens of guests. We served steak and all the trimmings, and finished with a chocolate mousse for dessert.

> Throughout those twenty-six years, Aunt Matilda used to come to our house twice a week, on Wednesdays and Saturdays. When she came, we had a huge party, with dozens of guests. We served steak and all the trimmings, and finished with a chocolate mousse for dessert.

The first example describes something festive, strange, and noteworthy; the second begins to sound like something tedious and nauseating. The reason lies in that small but ambiguous word "when." In the second case, we could as easily have used "whenever" (and it might have been preferable, though the preceding sentence contextualizes it adequately); in the first, the idea is quite different. Hence the difference between the general and the particular time. One can see that the general temporal construction is a bit more like a condition: " . . . *if and when* she came, we had. . . ."

English is not very good at distinguishing these two kinds of temporal clause in their internal makeup, though arguably there's no particular reason they *need* to be distinguished: context almost invariably steers us to the correct meaning. Greek, on the other hand, uses its elegant generalizing particle ἄν (for which there is really no literal translation at all) to flag the general temporal clause (and the corresponding condition—about which more shortly).

Some of the other temporal subordinating conjunctions are considerably more peculiar in their deployment. We may not think a lot about how we use them on a day-to-day basis, but we have—if only subconsciously—mastered a complex grammar of such things, and any deviation from its norms will strike us as peculiar or even nonsensical. One noteworthy example is the word "until." It obviously refers to the time prior to some other event or occurrence, and running up to that point. But we seldom think of just how nuanced our use of "until" is. When applied to the events of the past, it's relatively open-ended:

> He continued to chip away at the supporting piers until the building fell down.

> The building did not fall down until the last of the supporting piers had been demolished.

It seems incidental at best that one of those sentences is negative and one positive: the function of the "until" seems more or less identical. Both refer to a particular time in the past when, presumably, the building fell down. There's no scope for a general reading of this particular temporal clause.

An "until" clause in the future, however, behaves quite differently. Here is an example from a particularly menacing Christmas carol:

> We won't go until we get some, so bring it out here.

This "until" clause is most commonly found modifying a negative main clause. There are counterexamples, of course—"We will stay until we get some" would fit the bill—but they tend to be the minority. There's usually some negative implication even in the positive version. More significant, however, is the fact that this also refers implicitly to an *indeterminate* event in the future. The blackmailing carolers are threatening to remain however long they must to get their payoff of figgy pudding.

The trick here, of course, is that it's not really so much about whether the overall situation takes place in the past or the future—one could come up with an indeterminate version of an "until" clause in the past. The point is that it is being viewed in a forward-looking way—a problem in *aspect*, which we'll discuss later in the general consideration of verbs. There is a significant, if subtle, difference between these two sentences:

> Caesar continued the siege until he had defeated the enemy.

> Caesar decided to continue the siege until he defeated (*or* until he should defeat) the enemy.

In the former, we are talking about a *particular* time at which the defeat occurred. It may have been the result of the same kind of explicit intention we find in the second, or it may have been just something that happened. In the latter, the defeat of the enemy is a kind of boundary condition or limit governing Caesar's intention, rather than the actual outcome, and it could (from this sentence) have been the case that he never did defeat this particular enemy, but was ultimately frustrated in the attempt.

In Greek the indeterminate forms of these clauses will be marked with the mysterious ἄν again, unsurprisingly; in Latin the clause of indeterminate time will resort to the subjunctive. Such clauses are, in that respect, very similar to conditions, which we'll look at next.

## If and then

If time is the great metaphysical mystery of human existence, the great strictly *logical* mystery is the condition. All deductive logical inference is based on the formula "If a, then b." This can be represented in logical notation as "a ∴ b" or "a → b" or in other ways, but its meaning is still somewhat elusive on occasion. In natural language, moreover, there are many kinds of "if," and they tend to engage a wide range of specialized conditional constructions. Even with those options, conditions can be exceedingly slippery.

"When" and "if" are not wholly different concepts; accordingly, the verb forms and framing structures required by conditional clauses parallel those used in temporal clauses. Conditions are more complex than temporal clauses, however, partly because there is at least one whole group of conditions that have little or no temporal analogue.

One of the things that makes conditional clauses special within the broader spectrum of adverbial clauses is the fact that they often exert a powerful influence—beyond the normal range of adverbial modification—on the main clause supporting them. A specialized vocabulary has consequently grown up to talk about conditional sentences as a whole: the conditional clause itself (the "if" part) is normally called the *protasis*, while the clause it's modifying (the "then" part) is called the *apodosis*. These terms, Greek in origin, are convenient if only because they are more compact than almost any other way of referring to the clauses.

The relationships involved in conditions are extremely varied. Conditions share with temporal clauses the free play of the *general* and *particular*. In that respect they are nearly identical. They are also highly dependent on context. I can say, before checking my wallet:

If I have a dollar, I'll give it to you.

This—without any further context—suggests that at present, as a one-time offer, I'm willing to supply a dollar to my interlocutor, without any strings attached, for some unspecified reason, if I have one in my possession. If I don't, nothing else is implied. The very same sentence, in a different context, may mean something quite different:

> If you catch me misusing my personal pronouns, wave this red flag.
> If I have a dollar, I'll give it to you.

Presumably this is an offer that is open and can be exercised at any time, perhaps repeatedly, but I'm not offering anyone anything at the moment.

The questions that arise about conditions along this axis of the particular and the general are therefore more or less the same as the ones that emerged about temporal clauses when we were looking at the visits from our hungry Aunt Matilda. It should be reassuring to know that the mechanics of dealing with both of them also tend to be the same.

Conditions have one capacity, however, that we don't find nearly as frequently in temporal clauses—and that is to project imaginatively into the realm of the manifestly unreal. It's probably easiest to analyze these conditions as a separate category alongside the particular and the general. Take, for example, the following simple condition:

> If the surgical tools were heated to a sufficient temperature, they
> were safe to reuse.

This can be contextualized in such a way as to make it into a manifestly *particular* condition:

> If the surgical tools were heated to a sufficient temperature, they
> were safe to reuse. Were they not properly sterilized, or was the
> patient infected some other way?

This presumes that we are thinking about the handling of a specific set of tools on a particular occasion, and making an inference covering only that occasion.

We can also have a *general* condition, which in English tends to show an identical or nearly identical form, though (again) context is the great determiner:

> In observing a series of successful and unsuccessful operations, I
> discovered that if the contaminated tools were heated to a sufficient
> temperature, they were safe to reuse.

This suggests the scientific study: "if" and "when" here are very close to identical. "*If* the contaminated tools were heated" is more or less interchangeable with "*when[ever]* the contaminated tools were heated."

Finally, we can have an *unreal* (or *contrary-to-fact*) condition:

> The spendthrift medical technicians routinely discarded their surgical tools after a single use. If the contaminated tools **had been heated** to a sufficient temperature, they **would have been** safe to reuse.

This version suggests that it did not ever happen; it's merely a suggestion about how it *might* have been done better or more efficiently.

The first of these examples, therefore, is largely *inferential*. It speaks from a position of the speaker's ignorance. The speaker doesn't know whether the sterilization happened or not, but is articulating a process of *deductive* (logical) reasoning depending on that point.

The second is analytical and really quite different in its implications. The speaker is not necessarily ignorant of what happened to the tools at any given point, but is positing something interesting about the results of the distinction, and doing some classifying in the process. This is a good deal closer to the processes of *inductive* (scientific) reasoning. It suggests a relationship (not absolutely established as cause and effect, but inferred from repeated observation) between the treatment of any given set of tools and a satisfactory outcome.

The third version is the really intriguing one. Contrary-to-fact conditions are the bugbear of traditional logic. Basic (nonmodal) logic has simply decreed them out of bounds. In traditional Aristotelian terms, *any* consequence may ensue from a demonstrably false premise. It is actually a valid inference (as long as I am not a fish) to say:

> If I am a fish, the Eiffel Tower is a lump of cheese.

It is *logically* valid—but, while curiously evocative, it is neither very instructive nor very helpful in most normal situations. In terms of the formation of the conditional sentence in and of itself, it is a matter of simple inference. That is, nothing about the phrasing of the condition *presupposes* its falsehood.

The contrary-to-fact condition, however, *is* phrased in such a way as to presuppose its falsehood. The falsehood need not be absurd or self-evident, as in the case of the logical fish and the cheese Eiffel Tower. The falsehood is entirely implicit in the use of certain forms. In English, we normally use the subjunctive:

> If I had brought my camera, I would take a picture of that tower of cheese.

Alas, this use is teetering on the brink, and one more and more frequently hears sentences like the following:

> If I would have brought my camera, I would take a picture of that
> tower of cheese.

This is still considered grammatically incorrect in most formal English. In either case, however, the clear implication of the condition as stated is that the speaker has *not* brought his or her camera, and that there will accordingly be no documentation of the alarmingly large tower of cheese.

It is not always clear what people think they are saying when they resort to contrary-to-fact conditions, but it's equally clear that such conditions play an important role in our imaginations, and that the human capacity for hypothetical thinking is all wrapped up in our being able to articulate ideas this way. We are not going to abandon them willingly, nor should we. We like to believe that it *is* meaningful to say—as almost any candidate for the presidency *will* say about a predecessor, especially of another party—that he or she *would have done otherwise* had he or she been president.

Just for the sake of completeness, it's probably worth noting that this kind of condition actually does have a temporal counterpart, though it's rather rare in modern English. It is very close to a condition in sense:

> When you durst do it, then you were a man;
> And, to be more than what you were, you would
> Be so much more the man.
>
> —William Shakespeare, *Macbeth* 1.7

"When" here is virtually convertible with "if."

All these contrary-to-fact conditional sentences are hemmed about with logical compromises and imaginative frameworks so subtle that we rarely articulate them. They may vary wildly with context. Consider the following:

> If Caesar had been conducting the Gulf War, he would have used
> nuclear weapons.

> If Caesar had been conducting the Gulf War, he would have used
> javelins.

> If Caesar had been conducting the Gulf War, he would not have
> crossed the Rubicon.

> If Caesar had been conducting the Gulf War, he would have crossed
> the Euphrates.

> If Caesar had been conducting the Gulf War, he would have had
> three heads.

Each of the first two versions of this sentence makes sense, within a certain frame of reference, though they don't make sense together. They clearly aren't operating in the same sphere of discourse. The first takes Caesar as the prototype of the ruthless military leader who seeks victory at all costs. What we understand it to mean is that if someone *with that kind of character* had been in charge of military operations in the Gulf War, this is what he would have done. The second just as reasonably views Caesar as a man of his own time, limited by the practical constraints of being a Roman military leader familiar with Roman armament. Which one is right? Neither is particularly more correct than the other, in absolute terms; each has a limited but distinct meaning to the person who said it and (presumably) the intended hearer. The contrary-to-fact condition may require us to suspend any absolute judgment on its factual correctness, but we can usually elicit some real meaning from it.

The third and fourth sentences deal negatively and positively with the prag-matic geographical constraints of being in Iraq rather than in Italy. While the last sentence is unimpeachable on the terms of straightforward propositional logic, we will still take away the sense that, unlike the others, it's random and irrelevant to any sphere of discourse we're likely to identify.

Most common human use of language would allow that the first two sentences are meaningful—even if we cannot clearly define their respective boundaries, and that the third and fourth are of limited but particular utility in certain contexts. The last is unlikely to enter rational conversation unless someone is specifically seeking out some intrinsic absurdity.

To sum up, then: we have so far encountered conditions of particular reality, of general reality, and (specific or general) unreality. Different languages have dif-ferent degrees to which they acknowledge or mark the distinction between gen-eral and particular conditions in the past and present. In English, it's mostly done contextually, as we have seen; in Latin, situations vary somewhat; in Greek, there are distinct forms of the condition reserved for the general (using the subjunctive or optative moods in the present or past, respectively), and others reserved for the particular (indicative).

All of these forms get kicked slightly sideways when projected into the future. The future continues to support the difference between general and particular conditions, though everything tends to veer toward the general. Because the future is presumed to be contingent, future conditions, even at their most particu-lar, are necessarily a bit uncertain. The future does not support a contrary-to-fact condition—arguably because the future, not having happened yet, offers no fact to which to *be* contrary. For perhaps the same reason, neither is its particular quite *as* particular as that of the present or the past.

Still we are able to distinguish different degrees of future condition in English using various helping verbs; in Greek there are three distinct forms, and in Latin, two.

For the condition that seems at best improbable in the future, English speakers tend to say things like this:

> If I were to become a fish, I would be able to swim faster.

or

> If I were to pay you what you're asking, I'd go broke.

Both of these suggest that the condition is distinctly unlikely, and presumably is being advanced only hypothetically. Note that intrinsic possibility or impossibility doesn't have a lot to do with it: turning into a fish is not really something that happens to people in the real world, whereas paying sums of money is something that happens all the time. Still, the first seems to presuppose that the fishy shape-changing is not going to happen, and the second sounds like an explanation of a reason for not paying what the interlocutor is asking. For this, Greek has the so-called *future less vivid* condition, which is much like a future contrary-to-fact condition. The Latin form is also generally called the *future less vivid* condition, though it covers slightly more territory, and implies somewhat less about the likelihood of the event coming to pass.

A condition that is being presented as more possible or likely (whether it's really possible or likely or not) takes a somewhat different form:

> If I become a fish, I shall join the Olympic swim team.

or

> If I pay what you're asking, I will expect you to do a top-notch job.

Both of these treat the condition as more open (again, with no view to real-world practicality). In English we use the present tense of the verb, oddly enough, even though the condition strictly points to the future. Greek uses what is called the *future more vivid* condition for this, and it is accomplished with a subjunctive form of the verb. Latin will generally stick with the future less vivid for most of these.

A condition that is being pressed with real urgency—not necessarily likelier, but that it is in some ways more menacing—is a strong form that has no single equivalent in English. We may say:

> If you will pay what I'm asking, I will do a top-notch job.

But we are likelier to say:

> If you pay what I'm asking, I'll do a top-notch job.

Greek in this situation uses a very strong form called the *future most vivid* condition, and it relies on the indicative. It is also sometimes called the *minatory-monetory* (threatening-warning) form.

Latin as conventionally analyzed has only one future conditional form in addition to the future less vivid, and it's called the *future more vivid* as well; there is no future most vivid, technically, though Latin authors do vary the choice of verbs to heighten the sense of urgency. The use of the future indicative in the protasis is generally felt to be more intense than the more normal use of the present indicative, though this may express the influence of Greek.

While it's not the goal of this book to explain all the particulars of each grammatical construction in Greek and Latin, it may be useful to see these conditions set out in a tabular form. Figure 2 shows the Greek conditions, taking the future less vivid as something at least akin to the contrary-to-fact condition in the present or past. Greek conditions are introduced by εἰ or ἐάν, and some are marked with the ἄν in the apodosis. There is a certain orderliness about how they are arranged.

One must of course be cautious with any such systematization: because conditions in particular are flexible, and are forced to adapt to just about every corner of language and linguistic endeavor, they are constantly being stretched to accommodate new situations. Hence the "or equivalent" notation for the apodosis of some conditions in the chart: in point of fact, it could probably be provided

**Fig. 2.** Greek Conditions

| | Particular (Simple) | General | Unreal (Contrary to Fact) | |
|---|---|---|---|---|
| **Past** | εἰ + secondary (impf., aor., or plpf.) INDICATIVE | εἰ + OPTATIVE | εἰ + aorist INDICATIVE | Protasis |
| | secondary INDICATIVE or equivalent | | aorist INDICATIVE + ἄν | Apodosis |
| **Present** | εἰ + primary (present or perfect) INDICATIVE | ἐάν + SUBJUNCTIVE | εἰ + imperfect INDICATIVE | Protasis |
| | primary (spec. present) INDICATIVE or equivalent | | imperfect INDICATIVE + ἄν | Apodosis |
| | **Most vivid** | **More vivid** | **Less vivid** | |
| **Future** | εἰ + future INDICATIVE | ἐάν + SUBJUNCTIVE | εἰ + OPTATIVE | Protasis |
| | future INDICATIVE or equivalent | | OPTATIVE + ἄν | Apodosis |

almost everywhere. The apodosis is still the dominant part of the sentence—it's the main clause to which the condition is subordinate. If the semantic requirements force it into another shape, it will take that shape. Very often a conditional sentence may have something other than a simple indicative for its main clause. Here, for example, is one requiring an imperative in the apodosis:

If you have ever visited Greece, raise your hand.

Another might reasonably ask a question:

If Caesar has crossed the Rubicon, has he already entered Rome?

One doesn't tend to find these variations as much in contrary-to-fact conditions; even there, however, at least some are possible:

If Caesar had not crossed the Rubicon, would he have survived the year?

Latin conditions are similar; figure 3 displays them on similar principles. All forms are normally introduced by *si*, so it is not noted; the same basic rules and cautions apply. The chart is a generalization: one can uncover a nearly endless stream of exceptions by plumbing the depths of even a midrange grammar like

**Fig. 3.** Latin Conditions

| | Particular (Simple) | General | Unreal (Contrary to Fact) | |
|---|---|---|---|---|
| **Past** | imperfect or (aoristic) perfect INDICATIVE | pluperfect INDICATIVE or SUBJUNCTIVE | pluperfect SUBJUNCTIVE | Protasis |
| | imperfect or (aoristic) perfect INDICATIVE or equivalent | | pluperfect SUBJUNCTIVE | Apodosis |
| **Present** | present or (true) perfect INDICATIVE | perfect INDICATIVE or present SUBJUNCTIVE | imperfect SUBJUNCTIVE | Protasis |
| | present or (true) perfect INDICATIVE or equivalent | | imperfect SUBJUNCTIVE | Apodosis |
| | **More vivid** | | **Less vivid** | |
| **Future** | future or future perfect INDICATIVE or equivalent | | present or perfect SUBJUNCTIVE | Protasis |
| | future INDICATIVE or equivalent | | present SUBJUNCTIVE or equivalent | Apodosis |

Allen and Greenough. In these, as in all other cases, the syntax exists to serve the semantic requirements of the speaker.

Some features of these charts may be obscure to you, depending on where you are in your study of Latin and Greek. Make of them such use as you can, and plug in the other pieces as you learn them. Much of what needs to be said about verbs will be discussed in later chapters.

All in all, therefore, the landscape of the condition in any language is likely to be fairly complex, because conditions come in so many different varieties, and with so many different possible nuances of expression.

### Even if

A concession is a kind of condition with an attitude, we might say. The foregoing section should have convinced you that *all* conditions have some sort of attitude, but the point of a concession is that the apodosis (which is, you will remember, the clause on which the condition depends) is in some way unexpected or unusual in light of the condition. Concessions are usually introduced by a conjunction expressing that relationship:

> Though it was raining, the soccer team was playing.

The conjunction is sometimes reinforced with a word like "even": "Even though . . . " In fact, though, it's just a special kind of condition. With an "even," we can deploy an "if." The meaning of the sentence

> Even if it was raining, the soccer team was playing.

is not markedly different from the above. The two can be distinguished when it's necessary, but it's not a large distinction.

A concessive clause can contribute to the logic, balance, and rhetorical flow of a piece. A deftly placed concessive clause may disarm objections before they arise. It's a useful tool to have in your grammatical toolbox, but it seldom exhibits any very colorful behavior that can't be explained by the general rules governing the wider class of conditions.

## Where?

"Where" is one of those basic categories of thought that can be handled a number of ways in almost any language. One of the things that makes it hard to describe or analyze is the simple fact that we are so accustomed to using these forms almost interchangeably that we don't think much about them.

In fact, *most* of the time you need to specify where something happened, you don't need a clause. A simple adverb or adjective (or an adverbial or adjectival prepositional phrase) will usually do the trick. For example,

> Inside the town, everything was quiet.

or

> Everything was quiet inside the town.

Here we have just an adverbial phrase. "Inside the town" modifies "was quiet." A slight change of emphasis, though, makes it adjectival:

> Everything inside the town was quiet.

Here "inside the town" is being used to modify "everything." Few English readers or writers will notice the change. In Greek these distinctions are much more pointed, because phrases placed in *attributive position* with respect to a noun—that is, between the article and the noun proper—tend to take on a wholly adjectival force. Neither of those, however, is a clause—nor are most of the other ways of talking about such things.

In fact, most of the clauses used to answer the question *where* in English, Latin, or Greek are adverbial relative clauses. This quirky class tends to undermine what you think you know about relative clauses (and we'll talk about the other kind in the next chapter), since most relative clauses are adjectival. But these are the ones that use not a pronoun but a relative *adverb* like "where" or the like:

> The railroad station was built where the two lines converged.

Here, the relative adverbial clause "where the two lines converged" is modifying no antecedent in the main clause: it's modifying the verb "was built." Similar constructions occur in Latin and in Greek, of course, because it really is necessary and useful to be able to say things like this. Such relative adverbs are dealt with systematically in most basic grammars.

## How and how much?

"How" is a complex word and idea; it can express either the means by which something is done or the manner in which it is done. Comparative clauses cover the latter, primarily: the *way* in which something happens. They can easily be analyzed as comparative clauses of similarity, rather than dissimilarity. In English, they can be introduced with words like "as" or "the way":

> He ran the way a gazelle runs.

Manner clauses shade gradually into conditions; especially if the underlying comparison is contrary to fact, English is likely to include "if":

> He looked as if he had eaten a sour lemon.

Presumably the person in question hadn't *actually* eaten a lemon, though the possibility is not absolutely rejected. This can probably be analyzed as follows:

> He looked as [he would have looked] if he had eaten a sour lemon.

Nonequivalent comparative clauses are usually introduced in English by "than":

> He ran more swiftly than a gazelle runs.
> I have less money than he has.

Often these constructions are truncated in the execution, and so don't constitute full clauses:

> He ran more swiftly than a gazelle.
> I have less money than he.

But the idea of the clause is usually there implicitly beneath the surface, though colloquial usage sometimes subverts it. One will commonly see this:

> I have less money than him.

The latter would strictly mean, "I have less money than [I have] him." Exactly how that would work is hard to figure out. In contemporary English, however, this usage is becoming more and more commonly accepted, to the point that some dictionaries will claim that "than" is a preposition rather than just a conjunction. Its place among the other (strictly adverbial) prepositions is hard to reconcile on either historical or semantic principles, but the usage is gaining ground.

Again, these clauses can slide imperceptibly into conditions:

> He ran more swiftly than if his house had been on fire.

These once again can be "filled in" and analyzed:

> He ran more swiftly than [he would have run] if his house had been on fire.

Greek and Latin handle these issues in a variety of ways. Comparisons not involving clauses or clause-like structures are discussed among the noun constructions: comparisons of things don't always require clauses to do their jobs. It's less certainly the case in English.

In Greek, comparative clauses of manner are most often introduced by a simple ὡς, ὅπως, ᾗ, ὅπῃ, or ᾗπερ, meaning "as," but other options are ὥσπερ (just an intensive form of ὡς) or καθάπερ, meaning "just as." Sometimes the principal clause may be reinforced by the addition of a demonstrative adverb (not strictly necessary) like οὕτως or ὧδε, meaning "so" or "thus." Other variations emerge occasionally.

In Latin, the relevant subordinating conjunction is *ut*, meaning "as," followed closely by *ac si* and *atque ut*, both meaning "as if":

> Cuncta ut gesta erant exposuit.
>
> *He explained them all as they happened.*
>
> —Livy, *From the Foundation of the City* 3.50.4

> Tu autem quod quaeris similiter facis ac si me roges cur te duobus contuear oculis et non altero coniveam, cum idem uno adsequi possim.
>
> *But for you to ask me this question is just the same as if you were to ask me why I look at you with two eyes instead of closing one of them, seeing that I could achieve the same result with one eye as with two.*
>
> —Cicero, *On the Nature of the Gods* 3.3.8; trans. H. Rackham

Comparative clauses of quantity or degree, on the other hand, are somewhat different both in their underlying idea and in vocabulary. They may eclipse or presuppose a noun that doesn't actually appear:

> But my mother, frightened as she was, would not consent to take a fraction more **than was due to her** and was obstinately unwilling to be content with less.
>
> —Robert Louis Stevenson, *Treasure Island*,
> chap. 4, "The Sea Chest"

In Greek, quantitative comparative clauses are most commonly introduced by ὅσῳ or ὅσον, which may be (somewhat mechanically) translated as "in proportion as," though arguably Greek speakers understood them as something more fundamental and similar to our (generally technical) usage of "as" in mathematical or logical writing, when we say:

> The value of x varies as y.
>
> *(I.e., X varies in proportion to y.)*

Most often in such cases one will encounter a correlative "flag" demonstrative in the main clause—τοσούτῳ or τοσοῦτον.

The range of constructions available in Latin is similar. Latin is fond of correlatives, so you will find *tantum . . . ut . . .* (so much . . . that . . .), *tantum . . . quantum . . .* (so/as much . . . as . . .), and so on more frequently than not.

Greek, like Latin, uses the pronominal adjective (relative adjective, if you think of it that way) ὅσος (so much) in the subordinate clause, correlating sometimes with τοσοῦτος in the main clause. Often it covers much the same domain as a relative clause. This use of "as many as" falls oddly on the ears of modern English-speakers, but it is reasonably understandable, and its precision can become quite appealing as one gets used to these correlative formulas:

> . . . καὶ χαλεπώτεροι ἔσονται ὅσῳ νεώτεροί εἰσιν . . .
>
> *. . . and they will be the more difficult [according] as they are younger . . .*
>
> —Plato, *Apology* 39d

## How . . . !

Adverbial clauses are, properly speaking, subordinate by nature, but one form at least has escaped the bounds of this constraint and become a freestanding sentence—or pseudosentence. This is the exclamatory formula:

> How quickly he runs!
>
> What a piece of work is a man! how noble in reason!
> how infinite in faculty! in form and moving how
> express and admirable! in action how like an angel!
> in apprehension how like a god!
>
> —William Shakespeare, *Hamlet* 2.2

What is normally a subordinate structure stands alone as a complete utterance, though calling it a sentence strains the definition of the term rather severely. All languages have their borderline cases.

Latin accomplishes the same thing in almost the same way, with *quam:*

> Quam pulchra est!
>
> *How beautiful she is!*

Greek relies largely on ὡς for this task. In many other situations, ὡς and ὅτι can be used more or less interchangeably, but that isn't the case here:

ὡς ἄνοον κραδίην ἔχες

*How foolish a heart you had!*

—Homer, Iliad 21.441

ὡς ἀστεῖος, ἔφη, ὁ ἄνθρωπος.

*How urbane, he said, the person [is]!*

*(I.e., What a charming fellow he is!)*

—Plato, *Phaedo* 116d

Some grammars (e.g., *Allen and Greenough's New Latin Grammar*) present four kinds of sentence: statements, questions, commands, and exclamations. Arguably the last of these is a label of convenience: it can only be doubtfully analyzed as a sentence the way the others are.

# CHAPTER 4

# Adjectival Clauses—Relatively Speaking

*Of which there is really only one kind, for a change*

It should not come as a surprise at this point that adjectival clauses take the place of adjectives in a sentence or a clause. In fact, they tend to be among the simplest kinds of clause in conception, though there are some quirks about how they're built that will keep you on your toes.

## The normal relative clause

We call them adjectival clauses here because that's their function, but most of the time they're called by the more common name "relative clauses." Strictly, that's a problem, because (as you saw in the previous chapter) there are actually also adverbial relative clauses—those depending on relative adverbs like "where" and "how." We'll focus now on the adjectival relative clauses, which are the more common. They have an interesting structure, a very orderly disposition, and have, over the years, been presented so confusingly as to defy all reason. We'll try to sort them out more simply here.

An adjectival relative clause *as a whole* functions as an adjective, which is to say that it virtually always modifies a noun. Because it usually precedes the relative clause, that noun is called the *antecedent*—but in fact we call it the antecedent even if it actually shows up later in the sentence. It's more a logical connection than a strictly sequential one.

The relative clause is attached to its antecedent by a kind of grammatical hook. It uses a *relative pronoun* to stand for the antecedent *inside* the relative clause itself. You might think of it as a kind of strip of Velcro or a magnet, with which to attach the clause to a noun. The relative pronoun is that magnet. Once one understands how they work, relative pronouns offer remarkably little difficulty.

Deployment of relative clauses is a bit like a game of pin the tail on the donkey. You need to get it pretty close to the right place, or something very funny is liable to happen. Misplaced relative clauses, or relative clauses without clearly defined antecedents, may give rise to a certain amount of grim levity among composition teachers when they are grading papers, but they never turn out well for the student.

In almost every language that has adjectival relative clauses at all, the connection between the relative pronoun and its antecedent is established mostly by proximity—though the degree of proximity required will vary with the language. The sentence

The car **that** has a green paint job is in the garage.

does not mean the same thing as the sentence

The car is in the garage **that** has a green paint job.

The only thing distinguishing them, however, is the position of the clause. "That" is an all-purpose relative pronoun in English, functioning for singular and plural, for things and, sometimes, people. Like that magnet, the relative pronoun is going to grab the nearest thing it can find to attach itself to. If we apply a little common sense, that will be something that can actually be painted. If it's "car," fine. If it's "house," that's fine too. It's not particular.

In Greek or Latin, you have a little more latitude: because the relative pronoun is marked for number and gender, it's more particular about what it sticks to. It may leap over some intervening nouns that don't match up with that gender and number. Some authors—especially poets—are able to stretch the connection to a point well past the breaking point in English terms. Sometimes that makes a sentence in Greek or Latin difficult to turn into English, even if we know what it means.

In terms of practical tactics of disposition, it's worth remembering that a relative pronoun is always *within* its clause. This is more important than it may seem. In English it is very frequently also the first word in the clause, with the exception of conditioning prepositions that may help establish its function in its own clause:

The car **that** is in the garage needs new brakes.
The car **in which** the brakes have been repaired is now ready to drive.
A car **from which** the engine has been removed is of no practical use.

In Greek and Latin, therefore, there's more flexibility about where the relative pronoun goes in its clause, though it most often finds its way to the front. Still, there's nothing particularly surprising in the opening of Vergil's *Aeneid,* though to many a student it tends to foreshadow darker things to come:

> Arma virumque cano, Troiae **qui** primus ab oris
> Italiam fato profugus Laviniaque venit
> litora . . .
>
> *I sing [of] arms and the man who first came from the shores of Troy,*
> *[as] a fugitive from fate, to Italy and the Lavinian shores . . .*

Here the word *Troiae* (of Troy) dangles out in front of the relative pronoun, creating some potential confusion. It's worth noting, however, that it is *not* a word that is potentially a legitimate antecedent for the relative pronoun *qui,* nor does its position after the verb *cano* suggest that it really belongs in the preceding clause. The only valid antecedent for *qui* will be *virum,* "man," which is indeed what it's modifying.

In any case, the relative pronoun is a sort of hinge word—it represents the antecedent by restatement, allowing us to use it in a different grammatical function inside the clause. Therein lies its mystery and its power. Therein also lies a good deal of needless complication. Relative clauses have been obscured by an accretion of grammatical terminology that makes them seem more complicated than they really are.

If you have come this far in elementary Latin or Greek, you were probably taught that the relative pronoun derives its *number* and its *gender* from its antecedent—that is, the word it modifies in the parent clause—but that its *case,* for some mysterious reason, is derived from the use of the pronoun in the relative clause.

All that is arguably true . . . and yet rather pointlessly confusing. One can as easily and as correctly say that the form of the relative pronoun is always *entirely* determined by its place in its own clause. In that respect it's not any different from any other word in any other clause. *All* words in *all* clauses have to be square, first and foremost, with their own clauses, and they have syntactical loyalty to nothing else. The relative pronoun seems to be partly circumscribed by its antecedent merely because whatever the antecedent itself represents—the thing itself—isn't going to change into something else when you start talking about it in the relative clause. If we're talking about a fish, which is singular and (in Latin) masculine—*piscis*—then a relative pronoun referring to it is (in the relative clause) just another way of *saying* "fish"—and so it will be of course singular and masculine. It's not that the relative pronoun is connected by a spider web of complex rules: it's just that the thing it refers to remains what it is, and so we continue to refer to it in the same way. This should surprise no one.

Perhaps a brief side note about grammatical gender is in order. Yes, it's true that grammatical gender is largely conventional. The fact that *piscis* is masculine really does not reflect at all on the actual sex of the fish. A male fish is a *piscis,* masculine. A female fish is a *piscis,* also masculine. A fish of indeterminate sex is a *piscis,* masculine, too. But despite this curious disconnection between the grammatical construct and the reality of the world, the masculinity of *piscis* is apparently felt by native speakers somehow to inhere, at least to some degree, not merely in the word *piscis* but in the thing itself. Some occasional awareness of the disconnection will arise, and will create some comical collisions. No language is entirely regular—not even Latin, and certainly not Greek.

## Restrictive versus nonrestrictive relatives

A relative clause can be construed in either of two ways. Most of the time, we need to pay attention to context to determine which is which.

A relative clause may be *restrictive.* That is, it limits the scope of the word being modified. This sounds very abstract, but it's really not. Take, for example,

> The shoes <u>that I wore to the top of Mt. Everest</u> are worn out.

Here the relative clause *restricts* the scope of the general term "shoes." It adds something critical and necessary to the clause that's being modified. It tells us *which* shoes we're talking about. The mere statement "The shoes are worn out" is insufficient without that added information. The restrictive relative clause, therefore, is essential in defining an otherwise ambiguous term.

Relative clauses are used nonrestrictively as well. Generally called *parenthetical,* a nonrestrictive relative clause adds something of incidental interest, perhaps, but not changing the fundamental scope of the antecedent term:

> The shoes, which I have now thrown out, were too worn to put
> on again.

This doesn't restrict the term "shoes" at all—I may well have thrown out any number of pairs of shoes. It just tells the hearer another fact about those particular shoes (already identified adequately).

In English, parenthetical relative clauses are now usually distinguished from restrictive ones in two ways. First, they are typically set off by commas (or, occasionally, by parentheses). Second, there is—though the usage is by no means universal—a decided tendency to prefer "that" for restrictive clauses, and "which" for parenthetical ones. This was strongly encouraged by Strunk and White in their little book *Elements of Style,* and though the practice really has no historical force, it tends to advance the cause of clarity, and that's usually a good thing. At the same time, it is redundant in a sense. If regularly observed, this will lead to a double marking of the parenthetical clause—it will be set off by punctuation *and* marked with a "which." If this is a rule you want to follow, you need merely recall that a "which" typically follows a comma.

This is a distinction that naturally suggests itself, partly because we already observe it in the opposite direction. It's virtually unheard of to use "that" for a parenthetical clause, so using it where it *is* allowed will make the distinction clearer, leaving no ambiguity about what is and what is not restrictive. At the same time, however, there's no hiding the fact that good authors, from the earliest stages of modern English down to the present, can be found using "which" in restrictive as well as parenthetical relative clauses. Shakespeare does it; Milton does it; Austen does it; twentieth-century authors do it. It cannot be considered a cornerstone of English grammar.

It also has limits. The boldly declarative restriction announced by a "that" in the subject or object position in a relative clause crumbles when it's made the object of a preposition. It's all very well to say:

> The instrument that he played was put into a museum.

And it's clearer than this:

> The instrument which he played was put into a museum.

The latter could (at least in speech) be confused with its parenthetical sibling:

> The instrument, which he played, was put into a museum.

One can't, however, use "that" in place of "which" here, even if one is fully determined that it should be restrictive:

> The instrument on which he played Telemann's D Major Trumpet Concerto was put into a museum.

No native modern English-speaker would say:

> The instrument on that he played Telemann's D Major Trumpet Concerto was put into a museum.

Earlier English had a greater tolerance for such things, but here, as everywhere else, common sense needs to make the final determination.

It is also important for students of Greek and Latin to note that there is nothing overtly corresponding to this distinction in Greek and Latin usage. There is only one set or system of relative pronouns, and they have to suffice for whatever one wants to do with them. One cannot point to punctuation as any kind of historical validation, either. Written punctuation was not used in ancient Greek or Latin writing. Words were not even normally separated by spaces, for that matter, until the Middle Ages. (In 2000, Paul Saenger wrote an intriguing book on the subject, exploring this fact in terms of writing and reading and their intersection with neuropsychology: *Space between Words: The Origins of Silent Reading.*) Punctuation appears in modern texts in both Greek and Latin, of course, but it's entirely the product of modern editing, and editorial practice varies considerably on this score. Punctuation in classical texts is entirely a clarification of what the editors think the passage means.

None of which means that the *ideas* denoted by restrictive and parenthetical relative clauses were foreign to ancient Greeks and Romans. Greek and Latin relative clauses can be found with both restrictive and parenthetical meanings, and that's not particularly surprising. Differentiating them, however, involves catching signals from the editor (who, until you are at a relatively advanced stage in the game, probably knows the language better than you do) and observing the sense of the passage. In addition, in Latin (and, slightly less reliably, in Greek) restrictive relative clauses have a tendency to be pushed forward, into more prominent and intimate connection with their antecedents—sometimes even eclipsing them entirely (especially if they are indefinite):

> Qui cognoscerent misit.
>
> *He sent [those] who should investigate.*
>
> *(I.e., He sent men to investigate.)*
>
> —Caesar, *Gallic War* 4.25

> ἃ μὴ οἶδα οὐδὲ οἴομαι εἰδέναι.
>
> *[Those things] that I don't know, I neither think that I know.*
>
> —Plato, *Apology* 21d

A parenthetical relative clause, on the other hand, is much more likely to follow its antecedent:

> Aduatici, de quibus supra diximus, . . . domum reverterunt.
>
> *The Aduatici, of whom we spoke above, . . . returned home.*
>
> —Caesar, *Gallic War* 2.29

Inevitably there will be those cases where you won't be able to figure out which is which. Such is life: one muddles on despite uncertainty. Sometimes it doesn't matter much, either.

# Relative clauses that act like conditions

There are times and places where the force of a relative clause—the actual sense it conveys—is effectively identical to that of a condition. This may seem odd, inasmuch as the relative clause of a standard form is an adjectival clause, and a conditional clause is adverbial. This usually happens in general or indefinite cases; the pronoun is more or less invariably indefinite in sense (i.e., "whoever," "whatever") and very often in form as well:

> Whoso pulleth out this sword of this stone and anvil, is rightwise king born of all England.
>
> —Thomas Malory, *Morte Darthur*

> Who[ever] is not for us is against us.

These are not markedly different in sense from the following:

> If anyone pulleth out this sword of this stone and anvil, he is rightwise king born of all England.

> If someone is not for us, he [or she] is against us.

We tend not to think about the similarity of relative clauses and conditions much in English, but we often have to do so in dealing with Greek or Latin. Especially in Greek, the similarity has some significant ramifications, because the various forms of conditions (there are nine of them, as mentioned above) all can be echoed, in a way, by relative clauses, which will assume the corresponding verb forms, and also thereby take on the implications of the conditions on which they are patterned:

> ἃ μὴ προσήκει μήτ᾽ ἄκουε μήθ᾽ ὁρᾶ.
>
> *Neither listen to nor look at that which is unseemly.*
>
> *(I.e., If anything is unseemly, neither listen to it nor look at it.)*
>
> *(Simple conditional form)*
>
> —Menander, *Sententiae* 39

> οἱ παῖδες ὑμῶν, ὅσοι [ =εἴ τινες] ἐνθάδε ἦσαν, ὑπὸ τούτων ἂν ὑβρίζοντο.
>
> *[If that were so,] your children, as many of them as were present [but none were present], would be insulted by these men.*
>
> *(Contrary-to-fact conditional form with ἄν in the virtual apodosis)*
>
> —Lysias 12.98; trans. Smyth §2564

There are many other possible permutations—as many as there are kinds of conditions, really—and all of these are discussed at length and with great clarity in Smyth's grammar, §§2560–73.

The Latin conditional system is not quite so complex, and one encounters conditional relative clauses somewhat less frequently, but they definitely do occur, and they function similarly. A clause beginning with a relative pronoun or a relative adverb may easily slide into the sense of a condition, and the verb or verbs in such a clause will normally conform to what one would expect in the equivalent condition. These will range from particular conditions to contrary-to-fact conditions, or even future more or less vivid conditions:

> Quod qui faciet, non aegritudine solum vacabit, sed etiam perturbationibus reliquis omnibus.
>
> *Who[ever] does this will be free not only of disease, but also of all other kinds of annoyance.*
>
> —Cicero, *Tusculan Disputations* 4.38

This takes the form of the future more vivid condition. A contrary-to-fact condition would be shaped like this:

> Quod dixisses, certe audivissem.
>
> *What[ever] you had said I surely would have heard.*

This again is effectively following the verbal patterns of a past contrary-to-fact condition: it similarly implies that the addressee hadn't in fact said anything.

The thing to understand in all these instances, of course, is that while the syntactic pathways to these two kinds of constructions—conditions and relative clauses—are quite different, their semantic burden is very similar. Syntax, as always, exists to serve semantics.

## Connecting relatives

It occasionally happens in English (less frequently in Greek, and more so in Latin) that a sentence will begin with a relative pronoun that is *not* in fact modifying a word in the current sentence, but rather refers either to a particular word in the preceding sentence, or else to the idea of the preceding sentence as a whole:

> We must never again be caught unprepared by a powerful enemy. *Which being said*, we should begin to strengthen our intelligence networks immediately.

With a slight change of punctuation, the second sentence could reasonably be treated as a clause subordinate to the first; certainly "which" does not refer to any antecedent in the sentence in which it actually appears. Dictionally, this usage tends to create a sense of almost impetuous forward motion, of thoughts added on to previous thoughts as they have occurred to the speaker. However one understands it, though, it is a pattern that any Latin student will need to master. It is almost omnipresent, certainly in the great prose authors of the golden age— Caesar and Cicero both indulge in it routinely. One example must suffice:

> Quorum est talis oratio: . . .
>
> *Whose discourse is as follows:* . . .
>
> *(Speaking of the Peripatetics, mentioned in the previous sentence)*
>
> —Cicero, *Tusculan Disputations* 4.43

This is effectively equivalent to

> Their discourse is as follows: . . .

**CHAPTER 5**

# Noun Clauses—Form and Substance

*The clunkiest of the subordinate clauses*

Noun clauses are the least common of the subordinate clauses, and if one excludes forms of indirect discourse, they are really quite rare. In English, they mostly take the form of object clauses, though there are some cases of subject clauses as well.

## The slippery boundaries of substantive clauses

In theory, the boundaries between these clauses and certain others become somewhat murky. Allen and Greenough argue that noun clauses virtually always assume the roles of subjects or objects (i.e., they are equivalent to substantives in the nominative or accusative cases), whereas adverbial clauses can be seen as clauses that effectively reflect the ablative of the noun. I am personally more inclined to view the latter from the opposite direction, and say that the ablative case has chiefly adverbial functions.

Closely allied to genuine noun clauses are certain pseudoclauses—not actually engaging finite verbs, but doing their work with infinitives or participles—that accomplish the function we would normally assign to a clause. Under such a heading fall Latin constructions with the accusative and infinitive, including those following *iubeo* and *veto* and their kin, as do Greek uses of the accusative and infinitive, which are many. Most of the Latin constructions that work this way can take either the subjunctive or the accusative and infinitive.

Verbs of determining, permitting, decreeing, and so on work this way:

Permisit ut faceret . . .

*He permitted that he might make/do . . .*

*(I.e., He allowed him to make/do . . .)*

or this way:

> Vinum ad se omnino importari non sinunt.
>
> *They altogether do not allow wine to be imported to them.*
>
> —Caesar, *Gallic War* 2.4

In the broadest sense, all instances of indirect statement can be analyzed as noun clauses or pseudoclauses. The whole of the indirect statement is normally cast as the object of a verb of saying, thinking, or perceiving. Indirect command could come under this heading as well, though the shape of the subjunctive clauses used for it in Latin, or the equivalent in Greek, suggests that it is behaving very much like an adverbial clause:

> Proelio supersedere statuit . . .
>
> *He determined to refuse battle . . .*
>
> —Caesar, *Gallic War* 2.8

> Praeterea decernit uti consules dilectum habeant . . .
>
> *He decrees that the consuls shall conduct a levy . . .*
>
> —Sallust, *Catiline* 36

In either case, we are looking at the clause as the object of a verb in the clause on which it depends.

There are also clauses that are classified as substantive clauses of purpose and result. These are not really difficult to distinguish from common adverbial clauses of purpose or result; they are functioning, in the first place, as nouns, and usually take their places as objects of a verb entailing some kind of cognitive activity, whether thinking or wishing or striving. Clauses of striving and fearing are in some ways special cases of this general type. They are purpose clauses insofar as they express the cause or reason for the striving or fearing, though they need not express any deliberate purpose on the part of the agent:

> . . . nam ne eius supplicio Diviciaci animum offenderet verebatur.
>
> *. . . for he was afraid lest he offend Diviciacus's feelings by the punishment of this man.*
>
> —Caesar, *Gallic War* 1.19

In Latin, similarly, a subjunctive clause may take the place of the subject when the verb of the sentence is itself in the impersonal passive construction:

Caesar ut cognosceret postulatum est.

*That Caesar should investigate was asked.*

*(I.e., It was asked that Caesar should conduct an investigation.)*

—Caesar, *Civil War* 1.87

Greek has a number of similar constructions. One particularly noteworthy cluster surrounds verbs of striving or effort, giving us such expressions as this:

ἔπρασσον **ὅπως τις βοήθεια ἥξει.**

*They were arranging how some aid might come.*

*(I.e., They were negotiating for assistance.)*

—Thucydides, *Peloponnesian War* 3.4

The object clause ὅπως τις βοήθεια ἥξει is itself the object of the verb ἔπρασσον. Clauses of fearing in Greek work similarly:

. . . δέδιμεν μὴ οὐ βέβαιοι ἦτε.

*. . . we have come to fear lest you not be reliable.*

*(I.e., we have come to fear that you will not be reliable.)*

—Thucydides, *Peloponnesian War* 3.57

It's not my purpose here to categorize all constructions exhaustively: that's what a reference grammar, like those cited in the bibliography, is for. But if you go in forearmed with a general sense of how these clauses work, you're much likelier to find what you're looking for. Smyth argues (§2207) that object (substantive) clauses of both effort or fearing stand "in apposition to a demonstrative expressed or implied." It is not clear to me that this is absolutely necessary—the English equivalent may well presuppose such a demonstrative, but it seems clear that Greek was capable of taking these clauses as objects on their own, without any rationalizing demonstrative pronoun to support them. Either way, however, they should not be difficult to understand once one grasps what makes them work essentially.

## Indirect discourse of all sorts

Indirect discourse is the thing that seems to scare the most students when they are first tackling Latin or Greek. The concept in general is not that hard, but (as so often) the boundaries are hard to pin down precisely, and an added difficulty is the matter of tense. Indirect discourse is almost always introduced by some verb of speaking. The latter, however, is a broad category. It covers verbs of speaking, thinking, hearing, knowing—in other words, anything capable of sustaining a proposition as its object. All instances of indirect discourse are about what has been said, perceived, thought, or imagined; they treat a predication of some sort as an object in itself.

Indirect discourse can be broken down into three basic types: *indirect statement* (by far the most common); *indirect question* (probably the trickiest); and *indirect command* (occasionally problematic). English, Latin, and Greek all have different and sometimes complex ways of dealing with each of these three. Indirect questions are especially slippery: they often don't seem to the novice like questions at all. It's not really correct to classify them all as noun clauses—though they are normally analyzed as such in English, and all the indirect discourse formations have an object status that puts them semantically into the same general field. Because it's useful to survey all these things together, however, we'll deal with them here. So that we may have a firm grasp of the points of reference, we'll begin with the way these things are handled in English; from there, we'll go on to matters in Latin and Greek.

## Indirect discourse in English

### *Indirect statement in English*

Most of us—even those inclined to be intimidated by indirect statement in Latin—have been dealing with it in English all our lives, and find that in practice it presents very few (if any) difficulties. In English, instances of indirect statement are virtually always packaged up as noun clauses, which can be introduced either with or without an introductory "that":

> I say [that] we are well.
> I said [that] we were well.
> I will say [that] we are well.
> Beatrice said dinner was ready.

Nothing here is especially surprising. In English, we *adapt* the tense of the verb in the indirect statement clause to the tense of the clause on which it's depending—sort of. In fact, this is yet another place where English is a bit inconsistent. You'll notice in the first two examples above that "we are well" and "we were well" match the tense (present and past, respectively) of the main verb. They both convey, to a native speaker of standard English, the idea that the speaker is making the claim to be well at the time he's claiming it. The third example, though, doesn't follow this rule, for reasons passing understanding. If we want to make the report contemporaneous with the speaking, we *don't* say:

> I will say that we will be well.

To a native English-speaker, that would convey the notion that our well-being is projected forward from the time of speaking.

In order to point backward or forward in indirect discourse—that is, to report something that's referring to the past or the future from the time of speaking—we need to resort to compound forms using perfect or pluperfect verbs, or helping verbs of one sort or another:

> I said that we had been well.
> I said we would be well.
> I say that we have been well.
> I say we will be well.
> I will say we have been well.
> I will say that we will be well.

Again, the future variant slips a gear in the process, but it's at least relatively systematic as far as it goes.

English also supports what we might call an accusative-infinitive indirect statement, though we don't normally talk about an accusative case in English. It's generally assumed to be derived from Latin, and tends to feel rather stilted. It's used when one wants to affect a formal or Latinate style, or when differentiating particular subtleties of tense is very important:

> I said him to be a fool.
> I reported them to be departing.
> He said them to have departed.

None of these fits very naturally into English, and mostly their use is an affectation, but one meets them occasionally. In the more complex cases (like the last of the previous examples) they can seem very strained. In other situations, they're pretty common, and tolerated much better:

> He considers me a nitwit.

Such things were more common when Latin infused the learned English-speaking world more thoroughly than it does now. Here, for example, even the infinitive ("to be") can be omitted without any loss of meaning:

> Think we King Harry strong;
> And, princes, look you strongly arm to meet him.
>
> —William Shakespeare, *Henry V* 2.4

We'll talk a bit more about how these accusative-infinitive constructions work—especially their tense relationships—when we get to the Latin forms of indirect statement.

### Indirect question in English

In English we usually talk only about actual reported questions as indirect question. In their simplest forms, these are quite manageable:

> He asked who had brought the hot dogs.
> I wonder whether we are going to survive.

These are pretty straightforward, since they usually show up with a word of speaking or (specifically) questioning, and then something indicating the substance of the question.

There is a large class of other material that tends to be treated in Latin and Greek as indirect question, and which offers a good deal of grief to beginning students. Consider the following:

> I asked how many people were coming to dinner.
> I didn't know how many people were coming to dinner.
> He told me how many people were coming to dinner.
> I told him what the dinner would cost.

> When I know the gentleman, I'll tell him what you say.
>
> —William Shakespeare, *Much Ado about Nothing* 2.1

As we progress down this list of examples, we wind up further and further from anything that is really *obviously* an indirect question in the basic sense of the term. What we are looking at in all cases, however, is a situation where we have the answer to an implicit question, and where the answer is not itself given in the way the phrase is set out. The problem is that there are many subtle gradations of meaning here. At some point, as in the last example, the line between this kind of indirect question and a simple relative clause becomes very thin. How we understand "I'll tell him what you say," in particular, depends on the speaker's intention. If he means that he will report the facts that have been (incidentally) garnered from his interlocutor, then it's effectively a relative clause, and not an indirect question: "I'll tell him [that] which you say." If his intention is to report whatever the interlocutor tells him, then it's a true indirect question: "I'll tell him what[ever] you say."

### Indirect command in English

Indirect command is one of the simpler things to do in English, since we almost always just rope in an infinitive, and leave it at that. Since commands in the real world almost invariably point forward in time, there is not much potential for confusion on tense here, either:

> I told him to lock the gate.
> I am telling you to lock the gate.
> I will tell her to lock the gate.

As noted, the simple infinitive completes the job unequivocally and completely. One can also use a subjunctive object clause, however, especially with certain verbs of commanding, especially if the speaker wants to appear somewhat more courteous:

> I commanded that he lock the gate.
> We require that you fill out this form.

Here the "that" is less likely to be omitted, though it may be in some circumstances:

> I insist you pay us a visit this evening.

These structures are particularly worth bearing in mind because they correspond fairly closely to similar structures in Latin and Greek.

## Indirect discourse in Latin

The chief real problem in mastering Latin indirect discourse (*oratio obliqua*) is that the three types—statement, question, and command—take completely different forms. This can prove disorienting to students at first, though in due course all three types can become quite comfortable.

The more interesting issue with indirect discourse in general is that, especially in certain authors, such as Caesar, it can go on for pages, all depending on a single verb of speaking. At this point, certain other patterns for *oratio obliqua* appear, but probably the best place to learn those is in a prose composition textbook.

### Indirect statement in Latin

Indirect statement in Latin terrifies students quite unnecessarily. It seems to be rule driven and very mechanical, but once one gets the hang of it, it's really quite manageable. It tends to be extremely precise as well, which is always an advantage.

The dominant form of Classical Latin indirect statement is an infinitive phrase with its subject in the accusative. That's not a noun clause, strictly, since it doesn't contain a finite verb. It can be understood as taking the *subject* of the indirect statement as the *object* of the verb of speaking, and using the infinitive from there:

> Dico Caesarem venire.
>
> *I say Caesar to be coming.*
>
> *(I.e., I say [that] Caesar is coming.)*

The elegance of the system is its simplicity: the verb of saying is positioned however it needs to be in time—I said, I say, or I will say—and the infinitive takes its tense relative to that position in time. Hence:

> Dico Caesarem venire.
>
> *I say [that] Caesar is coming* (now, while I'm saying it).

> Dixi Caesarem venire.
>
> *I said [that] Caesar was coming* (while I was saying it).

> Dicam Caesarem venire.
>
> *I will say [that] Caesar is coming* (again, at the time I say it).

The infinitives swing from that point as on a kind of pivot:

> Dico Caesarem venisse.
>
> *I say Caesar to have come* (to be in a state of having come).
>
> *(I.e., I say [that] Caesar has come.)*

> Dico Caesarem venturum esse.
>
> *I say Caesar to be about to come.*
>
> *(I.e., I say [that] Caesar will be coming.)*

> Dicebam Caesarem venturum esse.
>
> *I was saying Caesar to be about to come.*
>
> *(I.e., I was saying [that] Caesar would come.)*

And so on. All the possible permutations can be spun out systematically from here, and the precision is virtually guaranteed. The chief obstacle for English-speaking students is the fact that the tense of the infinitive is relative to the time of speaking, and need not undergo *any* change of form to accommodate itself to that time.

The peculiar case in which the subject of the verb of speaking is the same as the subject of the indirect statement probably needs a little extra elaboration, especially since it differs so interestingly from the way Greek does the same job. In Latin, when this occurs (that is, when the speaker is talking about himself or herself), the reflexive personal pronoun (*me, te, nos*, or *vos* for the first and second persons; *se* [accusative] good for all genders and both numbers, for the third person) takes on the role. Hence if Caesar's original statement was

> Veni, vidi, vici.
>
> *I came, I saw, I conquered.*

his own later report of it could be

> Dixi me venisse, vidisse, vicisse.
>
> *I said myself to have come, to have seen, [and] to have conquered.*
>
> *(I.e., I said that I had come, had seen, and had conquered.)*

Someone else, speaking *to* Caesar, might say:

> Dixisti te venisse, vidisse, vicisse.
>
> *You said yourself to have come, to have seen, to have conquered.*
>
> *(I.e., You said that you had come, had seen, and had conquered.)*

A historian, writing about Caesar in the third person (or Caesar, writing about himself in the third person, as he so often did), would say:

> Caesar dixit se venisse, vidisse, vicisse.
>
> *Caesar said himself to have come, to have seen, [and] to have conquered.*
>
> *(I.e., Caesar said that he had come, seen, and conquered.)*

It's wonderfully systematic and regular, and forms a robust system. In all these cases, the use of the reflexive specifically assures us that the speaker is talking about himself or herself. If that's not the case, the reflexive pronoun is *not* used, and from that single fact we can understand that the speaker is not the same person as the subject of the reported discourse. If the historian is reporting that Cicero is talking about Caesar and wants to tell us that he has come, seen, and conquered, he will instead say:

> Dixit **eum** venisse, vidisse, vicisse.
>
> *He [Cicero] said him [not himself, but someone else] to have come, seen, and conquered.*
>
> *(I.e., He said that he [the other guy] had come, seen, and conquered.)*

The historical development of the accusative-infinitive indirect statement is intriguing and somewhat puzzling, because it occurs in both Latin and Greek, but does not appear in Sanskrit or most other Indo-European languages. Where it has emerged in later Western European languages, it is generally assumed to be a derivation from, or a conscious imitation of, Latin.

There are many nuances in Latin indirect statement, and there seems to be little if any point to merely transcribing an extended discussion of them here. A good Latin grammar will go through many variations with abundant examples. A lot of interesting features, moreover, crop up in extended *oratio obliqua* that probably don't occur to us very often, but need to be considered in an exhaustive treatment of the subject.

There *are* forms of indirect statement in Latin that are set up as genuine noun clauses with finite (normally indicative) verbs, much as in English. They are usually introduced by the word *quod*. They are rare classically, but they do occur:

> Scis enim, quod epulum dedi binos denarios.
>
> *You know that I gave a dinner [worth] two denarii.*
>
> —Petronius, *Satyricon* 71.9

In Late Latin—from a fairly early date—indirect statements introduced by *quod* become increasingly common, and by what we would normally classify as Medieval Latin they have become the norm. The Vulgate (Latin Bible) resorts to this kind of indirect statement as a matter of course, and its influence over the diction of the whole of Medieval Latin cannot be overestimated.

Even stranger, perhaps, such a clause can occur alongside or even embedded in an accusative-infinitive indirect statement. The typical question in Aquinas's *Summa Theologica* offers a response to the list of objections that appeared first, introduced by the phrase

> Respondeo dicendum quod . . .
>
> *I answer [that it] must be said that . . .*

Here we have a *quod*-clause embedded in an accusative-infinitive construction, from which (for good measure) the actual infinitive (the implicit verb *esse*) has been omitted.

### Indirect question in Latin

There are two problems in managing indirect question in Latin. One is just learning the right forms of the subjunctive to use—since we are no longer in the domain of the accusative-infinitive construction outlined above—and the other (and more difficult) part is learning what actually *qualifies* as an indirect question. This is the problem that causes students to trip up most frequently.

Dealing with a literal indirect question of this sort is easy:

> He asked who had come to the door.

It's reporting the overt asking of a question, and it's further flagged as a question by a verb of asking: if you don't recognize it by that simple semantic mechanism, you're probably just not paying attention. There are plenty of these, and they seldom give students any real trouble:

> ... ei, qui quaesivisset **quid primum esset in dicendo** ...
>
> *... to the one who asked what the first [most important] thing in speaking was ...*
>
> —Cicero, *Brutus* 142

But there are other sorts of indirect questions as well, and Latin makes particularly heavy use of them. Anything in which we refer to what would be *the answer of a question in terms of that question—even if it's not phrased as a question*—is likely to fall into indirect question in Latin. Another way of thinking about it is to determine whether the thing being referred to is itself known or unknown. This may be introduced by a verb of asking, but it can also extend to verbs of hearing, thinking, knowing or not knowing, and doubting or certainty—in short, virtually anything representing any sort of cognitive activity. Hence, though it no longer seems like a question, Latin would regard this as an indirect question too:

> I told him who had come to the door.

Once you really grasp this concept on its own terms, the idea becomes a lot simpler. One can, for a time, rely on the idea that it expresses the answer to a question, but even that's a somewhat opportunistic definition. Eventually one can come to a more intuitive understanding of what kind of clause will appear this way. Probably the better point to hold onto is the known/unknown dichotomy. For example:

> Sit denique inscriptum in fronte unius cuiusque, **quid de re publica sentiat.**
>
> *Finally, let it be inscribed on the forehead of each and every one, **what he thinks of the Republic.***
>
> —Cicero, Against Catiline 1.32

Here Cicero is not asking what each person thinks of the Republic, nor is he reporting anyone else asking—but the "what he thinks" clause is an indirect question nevertheless (and hence engages the subjunctive verb *sentiat*) because *quid* is a placeholder, like the algebraist's *x*, for an unknown value. It's the *answer* to a question, even if nobody is asking the question in so many words. If it were a known value, the whole would assume the shape of a relative clause, the relative pronoun would be *quod* (perhaps with an antecedent *id*), and the verb would be in the indicative mood.

### Indirect command in Latin

In extended indirect discourse where the verb of speaking has been left behind, imperative clauses will normally become substantive clauses, and usually of a sort that is broadly identified as a substantive clause of purpose. One might debate whether it's strictly a clause of purpose or something else. In construction, however, these clauses are not far different from clauses of effort or striving.

In a more restrictive reporting of a single indirect command, a great deal will depend on the exact verb of commanding used: some are happier introducing a substantive clause of purpose, while others are happier with the infinitive. These details need to be learned as lexical specifics, from a good dictionary:

> . . . his **uti conquirerent et reducerent** . . . imperavit;
>
> *. . . he commanded that they seek and bring back [to him] . . .*
>
> —Caesar, Gallic War 1.28

But this is also possible:

> . . . ad eum locum fluminis navibus iunctis **pontem imperant fieri** . . .
>
> *. . . they order a bridge of linked vessels to be built at that point in the river . . .*
>
> —Caesar, Civil War 1.61

A certain amount of flexibility is required. For the English-speaking student, the infinitive form is probably the easiest to comprehend. The substantive clause—be it of purpose or something akin to purpose—is the one to concentrate on mastering.

## Indirect discourse in Greek

Greek tends to complicate where Latin simplifies. It has not two forms of indirect statement but three. They can't be varied freely, however—one can't simply elect to use whichever one is most appealing at the moment. The range of options will depend largely on the verb of speaking we choose. In this respect Greek is not very different from English, where one might easily encounter

> I consider her to be the foremost expert in the subject.

or simply

> I consider her the foremost expert in the subject.

But we are far less likely to see the same construction with certain other verbs of speaking:

> I say her to be the foremost expert in the subject.

And without the infinitive, the same sentence would be virtually unheard of, and possibly not even understood very well:

> I say her the foremost expert in the subject.

### Indirect statement in Greek

Greek forms indirect statements three ways:

1. With the accusative and an infinitive (like the preferred form for Classical Latin)
2. With an object clause introduced by a conjunction (ὅτι or ὡς)
3. With the accusative and a participle

Figure 4 shows the most common verbs of speaking, perceiving, and thinking and the forms of indirect statement that each can take. Most can take more than one, and the pattern may initially seem fairly intimidating. In fact one need remember only a few rules: νομίζω and φημί (both very common) take *only* the infinitive; λέγω (probably the most common verb of speaking overall) takes either the infinitive or a finite clause. All the rest take a finite clause *or* the participial construction,

**Fig. 4.** Greek Forms of Indirect Statement

| Verb | Infinitive | Clause | Participle |
|---|---|---|---|
| ἀγγέλλω (announce) | — | ■ | ■ |
| αἰσθάνομαι (perceive) | — | ■ | ■ |
| ἀκούω (hear) | — | ■ | ■ |
| δείκνυμι (show) | — | ■ | ■ |
| δηλόω (clarify) | — | ■ | ■ |
| γιγνώσκω (know) | — | ■ | ■ |
| λέγω (say) | ■ | ■ | — |
| μανθάνω (learn, understand) | — | ■ | ■ |
| νομίζω (think) | ■ | — | — |
| ὁράω (see) | — | ■ | ■ |
| φημί (say) | ■ | — | — |

but *not* the infinitive. There are other verbs of speaking, thinking, and perceiving, but this short list will take a student a long way.

The Greek form most like the English form is the construction with ὅτι or ὡς, which mean "that" or "as." The reported speech following is a normal finite clause. Where it differs from English most noticeably is in how it deals with changes of tense. In English we say:

> I say that Socrates is teaching the citizens.

but

> I said that Socrates was teaching the citizens.

Greek (quite reasonably) changes the verb of speaking in accordance with the time of speaking. There's nothing surprising there. But in the interior of the indirect statement, it does *not* change the tense of the verb of the reported speech at all. The tense remains unchanged, and if the verb of speaking is in primary sequence (that is, time present or future, including the perfect), it will leave the reported verb unchanged entirely. In secondary sequence (anything in the past, including the pluperfect), however—in a very clear expression of the odd relationship that exists between the tenses of Greek and its moods—it will normally change its indicative verbs to the *same tense* of the optative mood. Hence:

λέγω ὅτι ὁ Σωκράτης τοὺς πολίτας παιδεύει.

*I say that Socrates is teaching the citizens.*

but

εἶπον ὅτι ὁ Σωκράτης τοὺς πολίτας παιδεύοι.

*I said that Socrates was teaching the citizens.*

To make matters all the odder, there are occasions when this latter convention is disregarded, and the indicative verb is not changed at all. This so-called *retained indicative* usually suggests greater emphasis or urgency. There's no direct way to translate that nuance of expression, but it might be rendered as follows:

εἶπον ὅτι ὁ Σωκράτης τοὺς πολίτας παιδεύει.

*I said that Socrates was indeed teaching the citizens.*

This finite-clause form of the indirect statement in Greek is not *required* by any given verb of speaking: it's always an alternative form. As you can see in the chart, only two verbs—νομίζω and φημί—do not normally allow it, though there are recorded cases of both using this construction as well. Accordingly, the finite clause is very versatile. It is very frequent with λέγω in all its forms.

The form of indirect statement most closely approximating the Latin is built from an accusative subject (functionally the object of the verb of saying) and the infinitive. The verb λέγω can be used this way, though it seems to prefer the finite clause; νομίζω and φημί are normally used this way. As in Latin, the tenses of the infinitive are entirely relative, and hence they remain completely unchanged by the tense of the verb of speaking. Hence:

νομίζω τὸν Σωκράτη τοὺς πολίτας παιδεύειν.

*I think Socrates to be teaching the citizens.*

*(I.e., I think that Socrates is teaching the citizens.)*

ἐνόμισα τὸν Σωκράτη τοὺς πολίτας παιδεύειν.

*I thought Socrates to be teaching the citizens.*

*(I.e., I thought that Socrates was teaching the citizens.)*

The third form of indirect statement is similar; its subject is once again the accusative object of the verb of saying, but the infinitive of the reported verb is replaced with a *participle*. It is not the most commonly employed of the three Greek forms, since λέγω, φημί, and νομίζω are dominant. But it's very broadly applied in another sense: it goes with a wide range of verbs of speaking, as the chart shows, but they all can use the finite-clause construction as well. As with the accusative-infinitive form, the tenses in the accusative-participial form are entirely relative to the time of speaking: they don't change with the tense of the verb of speaking. Hence:

ἀγγέλλω τὸν Σωκράτη τοὺς πολίτας παιδεύοντα.

*I announce Socrates teaching the citizens.*

*(I.e., I announce that Socrates is teaching the citizens.)*

ἤγγειλα τὸν Σοκράτη τοὺς πολίτας παιδεύοντα.

*I announced Socrates teaching the citizens.*

*(I.e., I announced that Socrates was teaching the citizens.)*

This may seem to be another manifestation of the Greek fondness for the participle, but once again it's not nearly as foreign to English as it may seem. We use something similar with certain verbs of speaking and perceiving, too:

The senator confessed to lying under oath.
Al denied having eaten the cookies.

The range of words introducing indirect statement is quite large in almost any language, and the further one gets from the most neutral (like English "say"), the more flexible and interesting the surrounding structures become.

While many would claim that these constructions are basically arbitrary, I'm less sanguine about that: I think one could argue that each one of them expresses a distinct mental model of how the matter of the report is related to the reporting, though it is entirely possible that these matters are not very near the surface of the consciousness of an average native speaker on a day-to-day basis.

There is one fairly subtle but interesting difference between both of the accusative forms in Greek and the accusative-infinitive form as it appears in Latin. You will recall that in Latin if the subject of the verb of speaking and the subject of the indirect statement itself are the same, the speaker is represented in the indirect statement by a reflexive pronoun in the accusative (*me, te, nos, vos,* or *se,* which would cover the same domain as English "myself," "yourself," "himself," "herself," etc., both singular and plural). Moreover, if the internal subject needs to be modified by an adjective or to take an object complement, that, too, will also quite reasonably be in the accusative. This is firmly entrenched in Latin: as a rule, even if the subject was not mentioned in the original form of the statement (i.e., if it was implicit in the ending of the verb or from context), it *will* show up in the indirect form:

>Caesar dixit, "Veni, vidi, vici."
>
>*Caesar said, "I came, I saw, I conquered."*

but

>Caesar dixit se venisse, vidisse, vicisse.
>
>*Caesar said himself to have come, seen, and conquered.*
>
>*(I.e., Caesar said that he had come, seen, and conquered.)*

This subject accusative *se* (or *me*, *te*, etc.) is not normally optional, though occasionally a Latin author will omit it when trying to affect a Greek style or tone.

This is because Greek *doesn't* do that. In either of the two nonclausal forms of indirect statement (accusative with infinitive and accusative with participle), Greek will routinely *omit* the subject if it's the same as that of the verb of speaking. More peculiar still is the fact that if there are adjectives or object complements referring to that *implicit* (but never actually stated) subject of the indirect statement, they will *not* be rendered in the accusative, but instead in the *nominative*. It must be emphasized that this happens *only* when the subject of the indirect statement itself is the same as the subject of the verb of speaking or thinking. How to rationalize this feature of the language is something of a puzzle; it may perhaps be seen as a species of *attraction*—which generally refers to the assimilation of the case of one word to the case of another, despite the fact that the logic of the grammar is in most respects against it. However we account for it, though, it's firmly entrenched in Greek.

This typically alarms beginning students, who consider it yet another irrationality in Greek contrived solely for the purpose of confusing them. Perhaps it is, though once again they might consider that English does almost exactly the same thing with certain of its verbs of speaking. We can have

>He said that he was the king.

or, more awkwardly,

>He said himself to be the king.

but we can *also* have

>He claimed to be the king.

or

>He admitted being the king.

These things are lexically specific in English—that is, they vary with the particular verb used. That's true of Greek as well. They aren't so alarming, taken on the long view, though they need to be learned one at a time. There is probably just no simple way of cooking them down into a simple formula.

### Indirect question in Greek

The indirect question in Greek seems bizarre to most English-speaking students, mostly because it is absurdly simple. In its simplest form, the Greek indirect question simply *retains the original forms*—person, number, tense, mood, and voice—of the verbs that appeared (or would presumably have appeared) in the direct version of the question. The range of things that qualify as indirect question, of course, remains the sticky part of the problem, but it's not very different from the pattern in Latin. At least the forms required are predictable and reliable, though they do need some massaging to get them into shape for English translation. Whereas English would normally say something like

He asked whether you were ready to depart.

Greek can say the equivalent of

He asked are you ready to depart.

This is jarring to many, but once one gets over the initial dizziness, it's very easy to manage.

Indirect questions can also follow the same sequence of moods as was outlined above in respect to indirect statement. The rules here are many and complex, and a thorough immersion in the relevant sections of Smyth (§2663–74) will help clarify them. A few examples may suggest the scope of the matter:

ἠρώτων αὐτοὺς τίνες εἶεν.

*They asked them who they were.*

—Xenophon, *Anabasis* 4.5.10

μήποτε γνοίης ὃς εἶ.

*May you never learn who you are.*

—Sophocles, *Oedipus the King* 1068

In Greek as in Latin, indirect questions may well represent something never explicitly asked as a question.

### Indirect command in Greek

An indirect command in Greek can be represented two ways—either with an infinitive or as an object clause, in many ways like those in Latin. These are not always—or even very often—classified as indirect commands, but I believe that it's useful to see them in that light, at least provisionally. They are also much like object clauses of effort (striving).

The simplest and most common form is as follows, representing a general form after verbs of desiring or willing:

> λέγω σ᾽ ἐγὼ δόλῳ Φιλοκτήτην λαβεῖν.
>
> *I say you to take Philoctetes by guile.*
>
> *(I.e., I say that you should/must take Philoctetes by guile.)*
>
> —Sophocles, *Philoctetes* 101

Somewhat less common, but definitely well-attested, is the clausal version:

> καὶ ἐάν τινα ἴδωσιν ἢ ὀφείλοντα χρήματα, ᾧ μὴ ἐπεξέρχεται ὁ πατήρ, ἤ τι ἄλλο ἀδικοῦντα, **διακελεύονται ὅπως**, ἐπειδὰν ἀνὴρ γένηται, **τιμωρήσεται πάντας τοὺς τοιούτους.**
>
> *And if they should see anyone owing money, whom the father does not prosecute, or doing any other wrong,* **they admonish him,** *when he becomes a man,* **that he avenge himself on all such.**
>
> *(I.e., . . . they admonish him to avenge . . . )*
>
> —Plato, *Republic* 8, 549e

All the forms of indirect command sit somewhat uneasily between this category and other general categories involving verbs of willing, desiring, or other mental activity. Real language has to cope with the reality that the human experience it represents is never as tidy as we would like our grammatical categories to be.

## Concluding thoughts about indirect discourse

It is not, of course, the purpose of this book to teach all the particular ins and outs of syntax in English, Greek, or Latin. Its main purpose is to demonstrate how these syntactic structures organically relate to the meanings they carry, and to encourage students to think about them in those terms. In the old English public school tradition, where masses of Latin prose composition were de rigueur, one might be expected to turn pages of direct discourse into indirect as a routine exercise. Viewed merely as a sequence of operations to be performed on a source passage to transform it into the target, it's gritty, grueling, and grim. Languages exist to serve and convey meaning (and meaning alone, if one considers the aesthetic pleasures of language, whether in poetry or prose, to be themselves a kind of meaning). Controlling meaning, of course, is no trivial task, and there is some reason to take signification, rather than mere reason, as the most salient characteristic of *Homo sapiens*. Perhaps that is a distinction without a difference, though: we reason by means of our signs—signs to each other, to communicate ideas and share them in community, and signs to ourselves, to help us keep track of what we know or think we know.

These signs include everything from the notation for calculus to musical notation; they encompass plans, maps, blueprints, lists, databases, and other external representations of what we know or think we know. They also include language. To grapple genuinely with language this way is to engage with the mind and thought that stands behind it. In the specific case of indirect discourse, neither the syntactic structures nor the structures of thought they represent are irrational or bizarre. Some are *different* from the way English handles the same problem—but that's part of what makes learning each new language worthwhile. Among these several forms of indirect statement, in particular, I think we can broadly discern two profoundly different patterns of thought.

It seems to me that the object clause is a way of encapsulating a predication as a discrete unit. Object clauses are normative for indirect statement in English, Greek, and later Latin. Because of what they are and how they work, they treat the whole idea as a self-contained propositional entity on its own. It's an analytical way of organizing things and of perceiving the world. It's a mind-set also reflected in the production of abstract nouns, or in the use of subroutines or library functions in computer programs. Such encapsulations can be unpacked at need, but may be handled without doing so if that's useful. That in turn promotes certain kinds of thinking, and it probably should be no surprise that the Greek language was the seedbed of what we consider serious philosophy, or that the rise of Scholastic philosophy in Latin coincided more or less directly with the evolution of the linguistic structures to support it.

Roman thought was otherwise, and Classical Latin expression reflects it. The accusative forms of indirect statement are conceived differently from the inside. Many elementary Latin teachers will duly tell us that

> I think the man to be running.

is entirely convertible with

> I think that the man is running.

Yes; both clearly refer to the same thing. At the same time, they really do differ in their *approach* to that reality, and that approach is part of the meaning being conveyed. The accusative-based constructions do not focus on the *proposition* as the object of the verb of saying, but on the *concrete thing itself*. What a purely mechanical analysis of the indirect statement may consider the subject is just as importantly the *actual object* of the verb of saying. That's a huge mental difference.

This is in keeping with a number of things one finds throughout the Latin and Greek languages and literature; they are less common in English, but not entirely absent. When Homer writes:

> μῆνιν ἀείδε, θεά . . .
> *Sing, goddess, [the] wrath . . .*
>
> —Homer, *Iliad* 1.1

or

> ἄνδρα μοι ἔννεπε, Μοῦσα . . .
> *Tell, Muse, the man . . .*
>
> —Homer, *Odyssey* 1.1

or when Vergil writes (perhaps in imitation, but perhaps as much from a general sympathy of perspective):

> Arma virumque cano . . .
> *I sing arms and [the] man . . .*
>
> —Vergil, *Aeneid* 1.1

none of these things professes overtly to be presenting *statements* about the men or the wrath: they profess to be presenting the men or the wrath themselves.

The Latin preference for concrete nouns over abstract ones also, I think, expresses the same impulse. It's not an accident or a mere linguistic curiosity that Livy writes not the *Ab urbis conditione* but the *Ab urbe condita*—it's not "From the Foundation of the City," strictly, as much as it's "From the Having-Been-Founded City." Thinking about it this way does something to your mind and your view of the universe. It's a good deal more than just the mere manipulation of grammar rules.

# CHAPTER 6

# Interlude—Some Historical Linguistics

*Where these languages came from*

One of the world's largest and most complex clusters of languages is that normally known as *Indo-European*. Its family tree encompasses several hundred languages with many more dialect variations; all the languages now generally spoken in western Europe, with the single exception of Basque, and many others across large portions of Asia, are demonstrably descended from a common ancestor, which most linguists now refer to as *Proto-Indo-European*. We have no *direct* evidence of the ancestral language: neither speakers nor texts survive. Its existence and features must be inferred indirectly, therefore, by comparative techniques, but enough is now known that we can actually say a fair amount about it.

The Indo-European family as a whole is largely divided into two groups known by modern linguists as the "Satem" and "Centum" languages, based on the roots preserved in each for the word "hundred." For a simplified chart of the Centum languages, which encompasses all the European descendants of the original language, see figure 5. The chart shows the family relationships of English, Latin, and Greek, along with French, Spanish, Italian, German, and the Scandinavian languages. The Satem branch, which is equally vast and spread chiefly across Asia, includes at least some of the classical languages of India (including Sanskrit), as well as old Persian, the Slavic languages, the Baltic languages like Latvian and Lithuanian, Armenian, and Albanian. Some of the world's most important languages today are not Indo-European at all, however: the Indo-European family does not include the principal northern Asian languages, such as Chinese, Japanese, and Korean, or the southeast Asian languages, like Thai or Vietnamese. Neither Finnish nor Hungarian is Indo-European, nor are the Semitic languages like Hebrew and Arabic. None of the native languages of Africa or the Americas is Indo-European.

Nevertheless, the Indo-European language family is an enormous linguistic cluster, and a seedbed of growth and change. For sheer diversity and extent, it is

**Fig. 5.** Indo-European Languages of the Centum Group

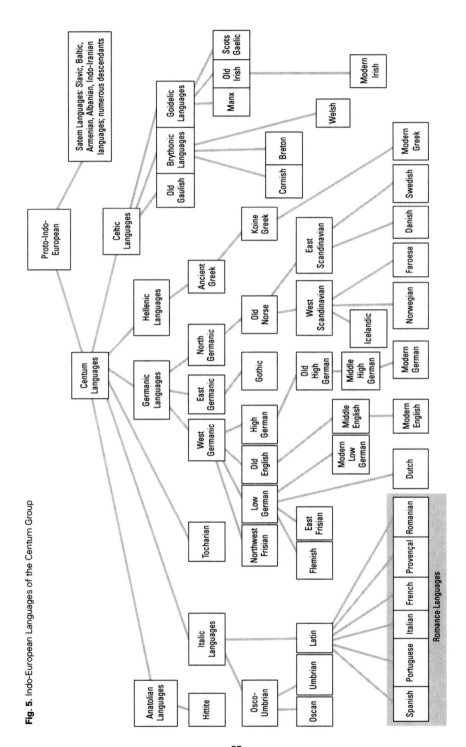

hard to find anything to compare with it. It also encompasses the three languages we're talking about here. As the first Indo-Europeans spread out across large parts of two continents, ranging from Britain to India, their ways of speaking evolved and diverged. In an age before radio, television, or even written texts, populations spreading out across multiple continents broke into isolated communities of speakers with little if any contact with each other. It is no surprise that changes occurred in the languages they spoke. What is interesting is that we can still say useful things about *how* these languages changed, and a disciplined examination of those changes can disclose a good deal of information about the ancestral languages themselves.

Languages change in a number of ways. They change in the kinds of ideas they attempt to convey, and they will occasionally develop new structures for saying new things. Profound notions, often so abstract as to be nearly impossible to articulate—like that of the direct object—in fact appear to have entered many of these languages relatively late in the course of their development. But in fact such deep transformations are relatively rare. *Most* language change takes place at the lowest level—in the specific arena of sound production. People begin to pronounce a consonant or a group of consonants differently, changing where in their mouths they are formed, or the way in which they form them. They lengthen or shorten this or that vowel, or a group of vowels; they brighten one sound or darken another; they allow following vowels to affect the ones that come before, in a kind of anticipatory assimilation known generically as *umlaut*. (That this is now what we call the two dots on top of certain letters reflects its origins as a marker of that change.)

The capacity for this kind of collective drift in a population is not very well understood, and the fact that it has happened several times in relatively recent history has done little to clarify the problem. Sometimes it seems glacially slow; at other times it's shockingly quick. The so-called Great Vowel Shift transformed the way most vowels were pronounced in English between about 1350 and about 1700, but apparently it took hold in most parts of England in little more than a single generation—to such a degree that it rendered regional dialects of English that were mutually comprehensible at one time virtually incomprehensible fifty years later.

What we do know is that there is a tendency for language sounds to undergo systematic, rather than random, changes in a community of speakers. Accordingly, for example, as the Germanic languages split off from the rest, they tended to replace whole classes of sounds with other sounds with a different manner of articulation. The primary voiceless *stops* (consonants like *p*, *t*, and *k*—so called because they represent a complete stop in the flow of air) were changed into their fricative equivalents (*f*, *th*, and *ch*/*h*). Hence the word that shows up in Sanskrit as *pipar* and comes into Latin as *piper*, in turn giving us French *poivre*, goes into German from its ancestors as *Pfeffer*. The word that gave rise to Latin *pater* came into the Germanic languages to produce German *Vater* and English *father*. The *p* has become *f* (German *v* has the sound of English *f*), and the *t* has become *th* in English.

Language differentiation through sound change has been fairly well worked over by historical linguists for the last 250 years or so. What has not been explored nearly as thoroughly, however, is the fact that languages seem to show an evolution of syntactic patterns as well. There is some reason to approach the very idea with some skepticism. Nevertheless, though language is constantly changing, especially in large and spreading populations, and even though it seems as if every generation treats the grammar of its parents' generation with gross disregard, I would argue that in fact syntax is for the most part remarkably conservative. This means that if we are careful, and especially if we have several languages to compare, we can sometimes peel back the layers of development and at least tentatively explore the underlying ideas that gave rise to those structures. In many instances, this is profoundly revealing, and in some it will provide insights into some of the language's eccentricities.

Language change happens among people, and it happens through time. One of the simplest inescapable conclusions of that fact is that the *order* in which things happen will be important if we want to figure out what is intended. A few examples will have to suffice.

To pick a simple example from the domain of sound changes, we will better understand how Greek accentuation works if we realize that it was, in the main, fixed *before* certain other sound changes occurred in the language. The genitive singular form of the common noun πόλις (*city, city-state*) is πόλεως. By the standard rules of Greek accentuation, this should not be possible. When the last syllable is long (as the vowel omega [ω] forces it to be), the accent cannot normally fall earlier in the word than the *next-to-last* syllable. And yet we have πόλεως. Why? Well, as it turns out, an older form of the word—the one on which the accent was originally imposed—was *not* πόλεως but πόληος. That is to say, the *e* sound was the long one (the letter eta [η] being long, while the letter epsilon [ε] is short), while the final *o* sound was short. (This also, happily, brings it into line with a whole family of nouns that have their genitive endings in -ος.) What is intriguing here, though, is that at some point *after the accents were fixed*, the two vowels underwent what is called *quantitative metathesis*. This high-sounding term means nothing more or less than just "swapping vowel length"—so that instead of dwelling on the *e* for two beats (*morae*) and for just one on the *o*, speakers began deferring the extra beat to the *o* sound, turning it from a short *o* (omicron) to a long one (omega).

Similarly, words borrowed from one language into another are almost never retroactively subjected to the sound shifts that have happened before their arrival. (There are some apparent exceptions, but they probably aren't worth dwelling on.) Hence words that enter English through French, say, retain the *p*, *t*, and *k* sounds that would otherwise have been lost. This can be confusing to the uninitiated, but in the long run it provides abundant and very reliable evidence for how and when a word arrived in the language, and actually enriches our understanding of the process.

I believe that using comparative leverage on the structures of syntax can enable us, in some significant instances, to figure out where certain different grammatical *ideas* came from, how they entered the language, and how to distinguish them.

Almost any beginning student of Latin hits something of a brick wall when first encountering the ablative case. Unlike the other cases, it seems willful and arbitrary. Some have categorized it as the catchall case; others as an example of schizophrenia in language. Arguably the latter is closer to the mark—but in fact if one figures out *how* the ablative got its meanings, a good deal of its mystery vanishes. The Latin ablative is far from arbitrary, but it *is* effectively two cases rolled into one, and these make much more sense as distinct cases.

The other side of this problem is that students learning Latin and Greek at the same time often find themselves at sea with the apparently weirdly differing constructions of the two languages. Latin has an ablative of means; Greek uses the dative for means. Latin uses the ablative for separation as well, whereas Greek uses the genitive. These seemingly perverse differences, however, melt away once one sees what stands *behind* these cases. In fact both languages, though they have modified the case systems they inherited from their Indo-European ancestors, are remarkably conservative in some other respects, and you can see that they are effectively continuing to use the same cases for the same things, when those simple changes are taken into account.

A little extra knowledge, therefore, of the origins of these structures helps simplify the surface phenomena considerably. This is the main business of the next part of this book.

# CHAPTER 7

# Verbs—The Engine Itself

*How the verb does what it does and means what it means*

As I said in chapter 1, the verb is the beating heart of any language. It drives predication of all kinds. Without verbs, one cannot say much of anything about anything. The verb is the essential piece of almost every predicate, and hence of almost every clause and sentence. There are clauses and sentences that technically do without verbs, especially in Latin or Greek, but when that happens, some verbal idea (usually a verb of being) is invariably understood. We talked about this somewhat above when we were talking about predication generally.

English verbs are fairly complex, but they are relatively simple compared to those of both Greek and Latin. Both Greek and Latin have large verb systems, and sophisticated ways of using them.

## What a verb is marked for

Whether in English, Latin, or Greek, we normally say that a verb is *marked*—that is, it carries distinguishing characteristics that help us identify how it is to be understood—for five distinct grammatical categories. They are conventionally given in the following order:

1. Person
2. Number
3. Tense
4. Mood
5. Voice

We will consider them in that order. These terms may be familiar to you from previous grammatical study in English or any other language, but don't give this section short shrift: there are things about Greek and Latin verbs that do not correspond well to what you've probably learned so far. In particular, Greek has a number of features that are not found in modern English or even in Latin: an extra one of everything, except for person.

## Person

What you probably learned about person in studying English is that there are three of them, and for reasons that seem fairly arbitrary, they are called first person, second person, and third person.

The first person denotes the speaker or the speaker's party: "I" or "we." The second person denotes the person being addressed: "you" (or "thou," "ye," or "y'all"). The third person is everyone else—"he," "she," "it," or "they." That much is probably familiar. A moment's reflection will probably serve to assure you that these three categories of people or things will in fact exhaustively cover everyone and anyone you have any occasion to talk about—you refer either to yourself, to the person or people you're talking to, or to someone else.

Greek, Latin, and English all use the same structure of persons in their verbs, and most native English-speakers would find it hard to imagine any other possible arrangment. In fact there are other person categories in some other languages—mostly having to do with subdividing the third person up into proximate or distant referents—but these don't encroach on English, Latin, or Greek.

## Number

Number probably seems as simple as person; we intuitively understand that there is singular and there is plural. What else could there be?

Well, in fact, the earliest Indo-European languages seem to have thought that there was a valid case to be made for another number category—what is now called the *dual*. It's reserved for things that come in twos. One can find the dual in a number of different places—if you look at the chart of Indo-European languages you will see that it must come from a very early stage, since it is to be found both in the Satem and in the Centum languages—it's present in Sanskrit, in old Germanic languages (including Gothic, Old High German, and Old English, though it was far from common there), in very early forms of Latin, and—most significantly for our purposes—in archaic (but still attested) forms of Greek, especially in the epic (Homeric) dialect.

Not everything that is two in number will necessarily be handled with a dual, though perhaps very early forms of these languages were more likely to do so. For the most part the dual survives into historical time in representing things that form *natural* pairs (two hands, eyes, ears, etc.) and things that *function* in pairs—a yoke of oxen, or occasionally a married couple. The dual is teetering on the brink of extinction even in Homer, and one will not normally find it at all in later forms of Greek. Even the Attic Greek of the fifth century B.C. has all but forgotten it, though occasionally someone like Plato will use it in quoting Homer, or to affect an archaic mode of diction. Most elementary Greek textbooks relegate the forms of the dual to an appendix, rather than including them in the main matter to be learned. As for Latin, the dual is virtually extinct in historical times, and makes almost no appearance except in deliberately archaic poetic diction or in very old inscriptions. It is still worth bearing in mind, however, if you're learning Greek: sooner or later you will run into it, and it's nice not to be taken entirely by surprise by it. It affects verbs, nouns, and pronouns.

## Tense and aspect

As a grammatical term, our word "tense" has nothing to do with tension: it is merely the Latin word *tempus* (time) as it reaches us through French (*temps*). We were probably taught that there were three tenses—past, present, and future. That's still more or less an exhaustive enumeration of the kinds of time (as such) that we can ever want to refer to. All time invariably falls into one of those three categories.

We may also have been taught that there are three perfect tenses, too—the present perfect, future perfect, and past perfect. Most beginning students never think to challenge that, but it's arguably true that those aren't *really* different *tenses* at all. Anything that is reported in one of the perfect tenses still happens in the past, present, or future. There are no other options. So why do we bother?

The reason we consider the perfect forms to be distinct tenses is that what we broadly consider tense markings in a verb are not merely about *when* something happened. That's just part of the picture. We use verbs in speech and in writing not only to locate events in time, but to describe what we might call the "shape" of the action relative to other actions. Linguists refer to this shape by the name "aspect." The essential fact about aspect, though, is that it is not something that inheres in events or actions themselves: it's a characteristic of how we are *talking* about those events. Moreover, it is about putting those events and actions *into a specific relation to other events and actions.* Aspect lets us express complex and nuanced understandings of how the various events in a narrative are connected to one another.

We can talk about actions as simple (just the fact that something happened); we can talk about them as things that are going on, but not complete; or we can talk about them as things that are already completed. In all these cases, the tense used is not just about how the action itself took place; *it's about how we want to describe it.* We may have various reasons, but usually they are controlled by their place in the larger fabric of discourse.

Consider the following:

> I was driving to school when I had a flat tire.

This is quite different from saying:

> I drove to school when I had a flat tire.

Even more peculiar would be the following:

> I drove to school when I was having a flat tire.

So what's the difference between these three sentences? The tense (in respect to time when) is the same throughout. Only the aspect has changed. The first tells us that I was in the midst of one action (driving to school) when another (the flat tire) occurred (relatively suddenly, one assumes—or at least I discovered it at a particular temporal point along the continuum of my drive). Presumably I set out for school with what I believed to be intact tires; somewhere along the way I picked up a nail or had a blowout, and that's when the flat tire occurred. The second sentence, on the other hand, suggests that the two actions were essentially separate and at least possibly unrelated. Only the temporal conjunction "when" tells us that they are simultaneous. To most native speakers of English, in fact, the second sentence suggests that the events are sequential, since there is no hierarchy established among them, and "when" is often used for events on which others are consequent. It therefore implies that I had a flat tire, or discovered that I had one, and thereupon set out for the school (rather a stupid thing for me to have done, but language can describe even stupid things). The third sentence is almost surreal: it almost suggests a slow-motion flat tire, during which I completed a drive. This is not impossible, if the flat tire was the product of a very slow leak, I suppose, but it is a peculiar way of conjoining the descriptions of the two events.

The point here is that we are using different forms of the verb not merely to locate events absolutely in time, but (more subtly) *in order to convey a particular understanding of the relationship of events and their consequences in time.* The verbs in both cases are equally valid. I drove to school, and I had a flat tire. How shall we put these two together? Most of us do this instinctively, but any nonnative speaker who bungles the connection will almost immediately identify himself or herself as not being entirely in control of the language.

In English, we talk about the "was driving" form of the verb as the *progressive* form, as opposed to "drove," which is the simple form. English also has another *emphatic* form of the verb, made up of "do" and the present form of the verb (arguably an infinitive without its normally attendant "to"):

> I did drive to school.
> I did have a flat tire.

The emphatic form of the English verb is not strictly a matter of aspect but (unsurprisingly) of emphasis. But the progressive form is there to establish something about what we call the aspect of action.

So what does this do for our understanding of Greek and Latin tenses? The verb patterns in Greek and Latin are normally broken down into "systems"—an imperfect system, a perfect system, and (in Greek, as well as some other older Indo-European languages) an aorist, which is a system of a single tense. The differences between the three systems are chiefly differences in aspect rather than in absolute time. They send ripples throughout all corners of the languages, and grasping how they're connected will considerably improve your experience in reading.

Figure 6 shows how tense and aspect in Proto-Indo-European and Greek line up with tense and aspect in Latin. Latin does not have a separate aorist system or

**Fig. 6.** Tense and Aspect in Proto-Indo-European, Greek, and Latin

| Proto-Indo-European and Greek Tense and Aspect | | Latin Tense and Aspect | |
|---|---|---|---|
| Imperfect System | Future (Imperfect) | Future (Imperfect) | Imperfect System |
| | Present (Imperfect) | Present (Imperfect) | |
| | (Past) Imperfect | (Past) Imperfect | |
| Perfect System | Future Perfect | Future Perfect | Perfect System |
| | (Past Perfect) Pluperfect | (Past Perfect) Pluperfect | |
| | (Present) Perfect | (Present) Perfect | |
| | Aorist (Preterite) | | |

tense, and this has several important ramifications. Let's consider each of these systems in turn.

## The imperfect system

The imperfect system, which includes the present (imperfect), the (past) imperfect, and the future tenses, functions in both Greek and Latin much as the English progressive does. Some teachers are so committed to this equivalency that they insist that imperfect verbs should always be translated with an English progressive. That's not a bad idea, about four times out of five. It covers most of their function, and if you followed the introductory discussion here, you probably understand why that would be important. There are, however, exceptions.

This understanding of the imperfect deals with it in a primarily narrative context, treating it as representing ongoing action as a kind of context or continuum in which to locate other descriptions of action. There are, however, exceptions. A few of the most important are noted here.

The *iterative* imperfect expresses something that is done repeatedly or habitually:

> The ancient kings used to execute traitors.

That is, they habitually did so. This is arguably just a kind of outgrowth of the idea of continuing action—it's not necessarily continuing without letup, but the process continues overall in keeping with an implicit pattern inherent in how we think about the action. Similarly,

> I walk to school.

does not mean that I am at all times or even at the time I'm speaking actually engaged in walking to school, but that I do so habitually or regularly—I did so last week, yesterday, and perhaps today; I will continue to do so tomorrow. The scope of the time signified here is of course highly context-dependent.

Somewhat less obvious are some of the other uses.

The *inchoative* or *inceptive* imperfect expresses something that is being begun. Beginnings (and endings) are typically related to things that are continuing, so this is probably not an enormous stretch of the imagination, but it does need to be remembered as a separate way in which the imperfect can work in Latin and Greek, since it is going to put a significant "spin" on the meaning of some uses of some verbs. (The present, being an imperfect tense as well, can also show this characteristic.) A few examples may illustrate the principle:

> iamque arva **tenebant** ultima
>
> *and now **they were just gaining hold** of the farthest fields*
>
> —Vergil, *Aeneid* 6.477

> ἐπειδὴ δὲ καιρὸς ἦν, **προσέβαλλον**
>
> *but when the proper time arrived, **they began an attack***
>
> —Thucydides, *Peloponnesian War* 7.51

The *conative* imperfect, which expresses attempt, is probably an outgrowth of this movement in the sense of the imperfect verb. Attempting to do something is virtually always (where intention governs the action at all) part and parcel of beginning to do it:

> Si licitum esset **veniebant**
>
> ***They were trying to come,** if it had been allowed*
>
> —Cicero, *Against Verres* 5.129

> **ἔπειθον** αὐτούς, καὶ οὓς ἔπεισα, τούτους ἔχων ἐπορευόμην.
>
> ***I tried to persuade** them, and I marched away with those whom I succeeded in persuading.*
>
> —Xenophon, *The Education of Cyrus* 5.5.22

There are a few other such applications of the imperfect, but these are the main ones in the indicative; the others can be garnered from a decent Latin or Greek grammar. The full nuances of these forms are complex and subtle, and need to be learned and savored over time.

## The perfect system

When one is taught about the perfect forms of the English verb, it's more or less conventional to explain them as having to do with *relative time*. That is, a pluperfect verb implies something that happened before another time in the past; a present perfect verb implies that something happened before the present; a future perfect verb implies that something will have happened before some (otherwise specified) time in the future. All of that's terrific, but it does seem to leave a gaping logical hole in the process. What's the *point* of having a present perfect if its only function is to express the fact that something happened before now? Isn't that what the past tense is for? Either of these sentences will express mere temporal priority as well as the other:

> I had a case of the flu.
> I have had a case of the flu.

But they don't actually mean quite the same thing, do they? The former is a report on some incident in the past. It may have been years ago. It may have been quite recently. In either case, it's reported more or less neutrally. The latter, however, suggests that there is something about this case of the flu that has some kind of ongoing interest. Perhaps the speaker is explaining why he or she is still weak or tired; perhaps he or she is explaining why the work that was supposed to be done last week didn't in fact get done. But the speaker is still, in some respect or other, operating under the shadow of that case of the flu.

That shouldn't really surprise us. Language is prodigal in its vocabulary; synonyms breed almost without limit. In basic structures, however, most languages tend to be economical. One will seldom find two completely different ways of saying the same thing unless there is in fact *some* difference in their meaning as well, and while many native speakers may have a hard time articulating exactly *what* that difference is, very few of them will confuse the two forms. We know our language in ways we don't know we know. In this case, there is a very important distinction, which will become even more important in looking at Latin and Greek.

The perfect tenses, both historically and in contemporary English usage, tend to reflect not merely priority in time, but the idea that the prior thing has, at the time that is the reference point (past, present, or future), some *enduring consequence*. This is the central fact about the perfect tenses that most frequently eludes students of Greek and Latin, and causes them undue fogginess about many of the other implications of their texts.

If I were to show up at your door (I wouldn't do so uninvited) at some unseemly and early hour of the morning, you might, if you were feeling generous, invite me in to join you for breakfast. If I had an empty stomach and didn't feel too strange about it, I might take you up on the offer. If, however, I had just come from the diner on the corner, where I had put away a plate of bacon, eggs, and hash browns, I would probably say:

> No, thank you; I have eaten.

We all understand the implication of this form, even if we haven't really thought about it. What it means is this: I have eaten, *and hence I am now in a condition of having eaten.* That is, I don't want anything more to eat. I could also say:

No, thank you; I already ate breakfast.

But (though it is possible) I am less likely to say merely:

No, thank you; I ate breakfast.

Why is that? The "already" in the former form points one in the same direction as the perfect. But a mere "I ate breakfast" could refer to something I did this morning, or even something I did two weeks ago.

Note, though, that the whole point of this is relational. It's about my response to your present invitation to breakfast. If I were a notoriously late sleeper, one might say:

You seldom get up in the morning at all! Have you ever in your life even eaten breakfast before noon?

To that, I could well respond:

Certainly I have eaten breakfast before noon. Why, one day just last month I had coffee and a roll at 11:30 A.M.

What's noteworthy here is that your question contextualized my response differently, so that now this is not a question about whether my stomach is full, but about whether I had ever had this experience. In this context, the perfect form is still appropriate, however, because it's still about a *consequent state*: it's about my current state of having experienced the delights of eating breakfast in the morning.

None of this, as it turns out, is new at all. In fact, it's one of the oldest things about our language, and herein lies the key to understanding the Latin and Greek perfects. Historically, and in most usage, the perfect tenses emphasize not the mere priority in time, but the *consequent condition or state*. If you grasp this point, you will have the Greek and Latin perfects firmly in hand.

### The aorist tense and system

The tense that we don't normally have, or at least talk about, in English, is what the Greeks called the *aorist*. The name "aorist" comes from the Greek *a-* (not) and *horistos* ("bounded"—the same root that gives us "horizon"). It's the unlimited tense. French and Spanish (and some other languages) have a tense, usually called the *preterite* (which just means "done" or "bygone"), that covers more or less the same territory. This is just a view of the verb that is more or less neutral in aspect. It *doesn't* attempt to put it into context with another action very closely; it doesn't imply, in particular, any relationship between the action or event and any present consequence. Because usually things being reported in this way are things in the past, the aorist tends primarily to be considered a past tense, but its aspectual range in Greek is much larger. The aorist can be used to cover all kinds of simple actions—or simple descriptions of actions:

> I had a flat tire.
> I ate breakfast.
> The American Civil War lasted from 1861 to 1865.
> The Paleolithic era extended till about 10,000 B.C.

Some of these things, it will be noted, took quite a while. That's not the point. The point is that *we are not attempting to draw a particular relationship between these events and other events*. This cannot be emphasized too strongly. It is common to suggest, especially in beginning Greek classes, that the aorist is a tense used to convey *point-valued* actions (generally) in the past, while the imperfect tenses (especially the past imperfect) are generally used to talk about *continuing* actions. But that's only half-true. The fact is that it really has nothing to do with the duration of the action in and of itself. It has everything to do with *how we choose to talk about it*.

There are other subtleties involved with the Greek aorist, and we'll return to these when we talk about mood. For now, it's important to know that Proto-Indo-European had an aorist tense that was used in this way. It is preserved in Greek. In Latin, something else happened to it.

Languages tend to simplify when they can do so without any appreciable loss in meaning. In Latin, the aorist tense converged with the perfect tense. The result of this is a curiously ambiguous sense of the perfect, which has confused students for generations, and which teachers have often helped to confuse by not understanding the difference themselves.

## The aorist and the perfect in Latin

Often, the Latin perfect is used as a simple past tense, much like the Greek aorist, or the English simple past tense. At other times, however, it is used as a true perfect—that is, conveying the notion of ongoing consequence. The *forms* are identical; the *functions* are distinct. It's important to recognize the difference between the two.

In 63 B.C., Cicero reported the fate of the Catilinarian conspirators with a sentence of a single word: *Vixerunt*. Any beginning Latin student who has made it past the third conjugation can probably tell you that that means "They lived." But is that really what it means? It does seem to be an odd thing to say about anyone. Of course they lived. We all have. Anyone you're likely to refer to has lived. What was Cicero's point here?

Cicero was not in fact reporting anything about the prior lives of the conspirators. Quite the opposite: he was reporting *that their lives were now prior*: "They are *in a state of having lived*." That is, "They're dead." And so they were: he (as consul) had ordered that they be summarily executed without trial (a breach of civil process for which he was later exiled). If one doesn't understand, however, that this is the actual freight conveyed by Cicero's use of the perfect tense, one can largely miss the point. Plutarch mentions that this formula was used to avoid ill omen by not speaking directly of death, but the import is the same.

In Vergil's *Aeneid*, book 2, which details the fall of Troy, Aeneas encounters the priest Panthus (lines 324–27), and asks him what is going on. Panthus utters the memorable and melancholy lines:

> Venit summa dies et ineluctabile tempus
> Dardaniae. Fuimus Troes, fuit Ilium et ingens
> gloria Teucrorum; ferus omnia Iuppiter Argos
> transtulit; incensa Danai dominantur in urbe.

One might naively translate this as follows:

> The final day came, and the inescapable time
> For Troy. We were the Trojans; Ilium existed, and the great
> Glory of the Teucrians; wrathful Jupiter took it all away
> To Argos; the Danaans hold sway in a city that was ignited.

But that would be to miss almost the whole point of the passage. The significance is all caught up in the nuance of the perfect aspect. Compare:

> The final day has come, and the inescapable time
> For Troy. We Trojans are no more; at an end is Ilium and the great
> Glory of the Teucrians; wrathful Jupiter has taken it all away
> To Argos; the Danaans hold sway in a city aflame.

Such an understanding of the passage is much more resonant and more evocative. Everything is about the way things are now on account of what has happened. Now is the critical time, the crux between the bygone and the new. What Panthus is talking to Aeneas about is the relationship between what has been and what is. This is not only much more poignant; it's also thematic throughout the *Aeneid*. To miss it here is to miss most of the point of the passage, and a good deal of the point of the poem as a whole. It's very far from being just a grammarian's fussiness: it's fundamental to the way the work means what it means.

This matter of the perfect aspect becomes relevant in a third case as well. It is customary for elementary Latin students to learn the forms of the perfect passive as posing a kind of odd exception to the normal tenses of the verb of being. The verb *sum* (an irregular) means "I am." This is fine. Most students learn it pretty early in their careers, and it has become deeply ingrained in them when, somewhat later, they are introduced to the forms of the perfect passive. Then they are taught that *laudatus sum* (the perfect passive is formed, as in English, with a perfect passive participle of the verb and a form of "to be") means not "I am praised" (as they might reasonably expect), but "I *was* praised." Some teachers will even tell them that in this peculiar case, *sum* means not "I am" but "I was."

This is balderdash. It's true that, taken as a whole, *laudatus sum* means "I was praised." But no change whatever has occurred to the verb *sum*. The fact is rather that the participle *laudatus* carries the force of the perfect tense/aspect. If one wants to understand it analytically (and correctly), it means something much more like "I am [now] in a state of having been praised." When one grasps this, not only is the riddle of why *sum* should change its meaning rendered irrelevant (even silly), but the true force of the perfect participle is allowed to come forward, and that, as it turns out, will have many further applications down the road—especially when the perfect passive participle shows up without *sum*. It always has that perfect sense about it. It will not do to forget it.

Because the Latin perfect tense, though, is effectively a combination of the Proto-Indo-European perfect and aorist tenses, one needs at every point to weigh just what kind of a perfect one is looking at. Just as it doesn't do to miss the point of a true perfect when it's there, it also doesn't do to impose that sense on it willy-nilly. Reading from context, with an eye always to the sense of the whole passage, is the only way to sort this out.

This dichotomy also manifests itself in the different ways in which Roman authors handle the perfect tense in relation to subordinate clauses. Subordinate clauses in Latin are normally subject to what is called the *sequence of tenses*. This merely means that if the clause on which a subordinate clause depends has its verb in a present or future tense (called "primary sequence"), the verb in the subordinate clause will be in one tense; but if the main verb is in a past tense (any of the rest, constituting "secondary sequence"), the verb in the subordinate clause will be in another. When the verb in the main clause is perfect, however, the verb in the subordinate clause can go either way: it will behave like a primary-sequence (present) verb if the author is using it as a true perfect verb, since the emphasis is not on the prior activity but on the present consequence. On the other hand, if the author is using the verb in the main clause as a simple past-tense verb (the aorist idea), the verb in the subordinate clause will be treated as secondary.

## Aspect in the Greek verb

The aspectual system for Greek is both more complex and somewhat easier to interpret, once one knows the rules. That is, there are more specific forms, but for just that reason, there are fewer places where one has to resolve an ambiguity, as one does in Latin with the perfect. Greek has seven tenses. Its three imperfect tenses are generally equivalent to our English progressive forms (though the future often has a simple sense—here true tense overrules aspect). It has three perfect tenses, too, very much like the true perfect in Latin. It also has the aorist.

To beginning students, the very idea of the aorist is occasionally bewildering. It's unsettling, surely, to discover that another whole tense has existed all this time, when you thought there could be only six. But its meaning is fairly easily defined, and most introductory Greek textbooks do a pretty good job of distinguishing the aorist from other past tense verbs. In their 1928 *Introduction to Greek*, Crosby and Schaeffer used the happy analogy of a still photograph (the aorist) versus a motion picture (the imperfect); others have used it since. That's fine, and fairly memorable—as long as one continues to recall that this is entirely about how we are *talking* about something rather than how it *is*. One can have a snapshot of an extended activity such as a race or a talk; one can have a film even of something of fairly short duration (though it is admittedly less likely). The same *action* can be given an imperfect, an aorist, or a perfect treatment, depending on how we are interested in viewing it, and in relation to what else.

The trick with the Greek tenses is that they tend to shift in their significance. Sometimes they function more as markers for absolute time, and other times they function chiefly to determine aspect. This varies primarily with the mood of the verb. Of the finite moods (indicative, subjunctive, optative, and imperative), the indicative is most concerned with preserving information about actual time. The distinction between the imperfect and the aorist is still strongly aspectual even here, but that's because they divide the domain of past activity on aspectual principles. But otherwise, the aorist tends to be a simple past tense, while the imperfect most commonly conveys ongoing activity, like the English progressive. There's seldom any real doubt that either one of them is in the past . . . except, of course, we need always to remember that in Greek there are always a few exceptions. Here are two.

The first big exception is that to make a broad statement about a universal truth—the way things are (for which both English and Latin will normally resort to the present tense), Greek will normally use the aorist. This quirky feature is called the *gnomic aorist*. It has nothing to do with comic statues on the lawn, but rather with the fact that these opinions or generic statements are generally called *gnomai*, hence "gnomes." In most other cases, however, the aorist in the indicative is usually reliably a past-tense verb with a simple aspect of action:

παθὼν δέ τε νήπιος ἔγνω

*a fool learns by experience*

—Hesiod, *Works and Days* 218

The second exception is that contrary-to-fact conditions specifically divide the domain between the imperfect indicative (not any form of the present) for *present* contrary-to-fact conditions, and the aorist indicative for *past* contrary-to-fact conditions. This may seem to resemble something similar in English, but the resemblance is illusory: English contrary-to-fact conditions with "was," for example, go to "were" because it's subjunctive, not because it's past.

Aspect dominates in the remaining finite moods. In the subjunctive and optative, the tenses have virtually no significance as descriptors of absolute time. They are all about aspect. As mentioned above, Latin has what is called the *sequence of tenses*; Greek gives this whole matter an odd twist, and distributes certain kinds of subordinate clauses between the subjunctive and the optative moods, depending on the tense of the verb in the primary clause. Hence the actual time at which something occurs is reflected not principally by the tense at all, but by the mood. This may seem inexplicable, but there are good historical reasons for it.

In the imperative, the aorist is used in variation with the present chiefly to distinguish between "do *x*" and "be doing *x*." That makes a certain amount of sense. There's no need for the tense of the verb to convey actual time in the imperative: it's always going to refer to the future. One only ever gives instructions in the real world with a view to the future. Even the often-heard "Do it now" really only means "Do it without delay."

With participles and infinitives, the game changes again. Tenses are once again more concerned with expressing actual time, but they've shifted the ground rules somewhat. In this regard they're like the tenses of Latin participles and infinitives. They convey not *absolute* time, but *relative* time—that is, time relative to the time frame of the main verb on which they depend.

# Mood

Just as tense is not about anxiety, so also mood is not about one's emotional state. We get the word from the Latin *modus*, and it really means more like what we'd use the word "mode" to mean today. Be that as it may, the word "mood" has caught on, so we are stuck with it. For all that it doesn't express (as such) a disposition or temperament, it does in some important ways convey the attitude of the speaker to the thing in question.

There are four true (also sometimes called *finite*) moods in Latin and Greek. The Latin student really will have to know about only three, though it's a good idea to bear the fourth in mind, in case one eventually decides to learn Greek, or decides to read Vergil or other poets of a Hellenizing disposition. The four, therefore, are the indicative, subjunctive, optative, and imperative.

## Indicative

The indicative is the simplest of these, and it's the one used in most of the examples, unless we're trying to prove some other point. It's used to make a statement, which is, after all, the simplest form of predication. It's also used to ask a question. Those two uses cover so much of what we have to do with language anyway that the indicative inevitably dominates.

The indicative is also used in Greek to set up contrary-to-fact conditions. This is one of the (relatively few) instances where Greek grammar and Latin grammar seem simply to be butting heads like a couple of bighorn sheep. Like English, Latin uses the subjunctive for contrary-to-fact conditions. But the Latin conditional system is significantly simpler than the Greek one, and this is one of those cases where simplicity is deceptive. A more fully elaborated system might well have been easier to interpret.

Both the Latin and Greek indicatives appear in some situations where it might have been normal in English to employ a subjunctive. We would normally say:

> It would be better to go.

But Latin would be more likely to put it more baldly:

> Melius est ire.
>
> *To go is better.*

This is a trend, rather than any absolute rule. Both options exist in both languages.

## Subjunctive

English speakers have an uneasy relationship with the subjunctive. It is clearly historically attested in our language, and there are a number of places where it's appropriate to use it, but they are poorly documented, even in formal English grammar texts, and many people do not use the subjunctive consistently at all; even historically it is sometimes misused (and sometimes by good authors, as far back as Shakespeare, at least). The subjunctive is on the retreat everywhere, and the result is a welter of other circumlocutions, many of which seem clangorous to those who have been trained in the more traditional usage. Today one often hears sentences like the following:

I wish I would have brought my raincoat.

or

If I would have brought my raincoat, I would not be so wet.

The forms, conventionally, should be as follows:

I wish I had brought my raincoat.

or

If I had brought my raincoat, I would not be so wet.

The "would" form is used legitimately in expressing the apodosis (the "then" part) of a contrary-to-fact conditional sentence, or something that would obtain if some implicit condition were fulfilled, or (historically) to express a wish; it is *not* normally used to express the contrary-to-fact condition itself. In this, English usage is somewhat closer to French than to Greek or Latin. The English subjunctive is enfeebled, perhaps, but it does express a certain nuance that is not easily accomplished by any other means, and it may cling to life for a while yet, if only for that reason.

The subjunctive gets its name from the fact that it is normally used for *subjoined*—that is, subordinate—clauses. That's a fair description but a poor definition, since it leaves some important functions out. Both Greek and Latin (and English too, to some extent) have sentences that are controlled at the top level—in the main clause—by verbs in the subjunctive (sometimes called the *independent* subjunctive). But it certainly is true that since the main function of the subjunctive is to express something that is hypothetical, it most frequently occurs in subordinate clauses.

One of the peculiar features of the subjunctive in Greek and Latin is that it has no future forms. Some students merely accept this as one more irrational fact among many, but there is good reason to think that this is because it is in origin kind of a "moodification" of a verb in the future tense. That is, there are no future subjunctives precisely because *all* subjunctives are, in a sense, aware of the fact that they carry a kind of futurity about them. The origins of all this are obscure, since they lie far back in the shared history of these languages, but as W. W. Goodwin points out in his *Syntax of the Moods and Tenses of the Greek Verb* (§6), "The subjunctive, in its simplest and apparently most primitive use, seen in Homer (284), expresses futurity, like the future indicative, and has οὐ for its negative." After some examples, he further points out: "Though this primitive use disappears in the later language, the subjunctive still remains closely related in sense to the future indicative, and in most of its construction can be interchanged with it."

All this hovers in the murky air around the subject of *contingency*—a difficult philosophical concept tied up with notions of fate and determinacy; we've mentioned it already. I certainly don't here want to get into the weightier implications of the issue, but in practical linguistic terms, it seems to have been the case that early Indo-European usage entailed the pragmatic assumption that what was future was not yet determined in the way the events of the past or present were. The most fundamental way to express that indeterminacy—the hypothetical quality of any event—was to co-opt a variant of the future tense to express it. The subjunctive becomes, ultimately, a kind of past future tense—something expressing the indeterminacy or futurity of something from the point of view of the past or the present.

This shows up most clearly in things like purpose and result clauses. We have already talked about these at some length. But if I say:

I built the house so that it would withstand the rain.

this means that I undertook the action of building with a *later end* in view. The result envisioned is subsequent to the action of building, and hence is seen as future at the time of building. The same can be said of the result clause proper. If I say:

He built the house so poorly that it leaked.

this again signifies a result that is subsequent to—in the future from the point of view of the time of building. In fact, all three of these languages deal with these things differently. English uses the subjunctive for purpose clauses but not for result clauses (like the one above), when it uses a clause at all: most often purpose is expressed in English with an infinitive of purpose. Latin uses the subjunctive for both purpose and result, spawning occasional confusion about what a given clause may be. An infinitive of purpose also appears in Late and Vulgar Latin.

Greek uses the subjunctive for present purpose clauses, but resorts to the optative in secondary sequence—either way, though, the verb form expresses contingency and futurity in a composite sense.

In Greek result clauses, however, neither the subjunctive nor the optative makes an appearance. Greek has two different result constructions, as noted above in the discussion of adverbial clauses in chapter 3. It distinguishes clauses of *actual result* (like the one just mentioned) from clauses of *natural result*. The latter refers to an expected or reasonable outcome of some action, irrespective of whether it actually occurred or not:

> The house was built so poorly as to fall down in the first earthquake.

It may well be the case that the building inspectors, upon seeing it, demanded its immediate demolition before any earthquake could shake it down. It's possible that it passed through an earthquake, and, against all expectations, survived. If, on the other hand, we are implying that the result was *real*, we would say:

> The house was built so poorly that it fell down in the first earthquake.

Like English, Greek expresses actual result with the indicative, and natural result not with the subjunctive or the optative, but with an *infinitive* of the verb. We'll discuss the infinitive later, but for now let it suffice to say that it is not one of the finite forms of the verb—and so it also means that while there is a true clause of actual result, the natural result construction is not strictly a clause at all. This is probably a mere technicality, though, since in most other ways it functions as if it really were a clause.

## Optative

Proto-Indo-European, and Greek in its wake, had one more finite mood that does not appear in Latin (though the language is in many ways more conservative than Greek is) or in the Germanic languages (including English). We call it the *optative*, from the Latin verb *opto, -are*, which signifies wish. In its independent uses, the optative does (among other things) express wish. When accompanied by the peculiar particle ἄν, it also expresses possibility. These two uses are significant, but it is in subordinate clauses that the optative truly comes into its own.

In many Greek subordinate clauses, the optative functions as a kind of second-tier subjunctive—a kind of metasubjunctive for clauses in secondary sequence. As noted previously, whereas Latin has a regular *sequence of tenses*, Greek exhibits a *sequence of moods*. The particulars are somewhat complicated, but any solid introductory Greek course will take you through them. They still all go back to the notion that the subjunctive is in some sense future in its primordial sense.

Finally, it should be pointed out that, like the subjunctive in modern English, the optative was on the wane already in our earliest Greek texts. It is reasonably strong in the Homeric dialect, and it remains important in Attic Greek. In the Koine dialect of the New Testament, however, it has become extremely rare, and is preserved only in a handful of more or less formulaic phrases, such as Paul's refrain μὴ γένοιτο, which recurs throughout the book of Romans ("may it not be so" or "by no means"). This is almost certainly a fossilized form, used much as a modern English-speaker who does not normally form phrases with the subjunctive might still use "heaven forbid." The use of the optative in subordinate clauses has almost entirely disappeared from Koine, and it has been replaced mostly by the subjunctive. (This is one of the reasons that those who learn Classical Greek tend to have little difficulty reading the New Testament, but those whose study has been entirely devoted to New Testament Greek will still find authors like Homer, Aeschylus, and Thucydides hard to understand.)

## Imperative

The imperative mood is the last of the finite moods, and it should be familiar to anyone who has studied English grammatical terminology. It's used for giving orders. In English, the imperative virtually always appears without an explicit subject, on the assumption that the only person you can really give an order to is the person to whom you are talking. If that subject is added, it's almost always simply the emphatic "you." Accordingly, all imperative verbs are construed to be second person.

Greek, on the other hand, supports both a second-person and a third-person imperative. The forms are different, and the third-person imperative often does employ an explicit subject ("he," "she," or "it" is seldom as unambiguous as "you," after all). There's no direct equivalent in English; in order to translate these, we need to resort to what we call a *jussive* construction (in Latin it's normally done with the subjunctive) meaning something like our "Let . . ." It often crops up in judicial language:

> Let him be taken from the court and hanged.

This third-person imperative is so routine in Greek that it is just part of the mental landscape of Greek authors, and appreciating that it really is a genuine imperative at its core adds a good deal of richness to the experience of reading it, even if it defies closely analogical translation into English.

Latin imperatives distinguish singular and plural, which means that there's another form to learn, but most of the time they appear in the second person. There is an uncommon but still occasionally important future imperative in Latin that has a third-person form. It appears in the ancient tables of the law and in occasional poetic usage, but it's considered curious and archaic by the classical period:

> Iusta imperia **sunto**, eisque cives modeste **parento**.
>
> *Let there be just authorities, and let the citizens compliantly obey them.*
>
> —*Laws* 3.6

It's worth noting that both Greek and Latin support alternative ways of giving commands *without* the imperative. One can give commands with certain forms of the subjunctive in both Greek and Latin, and both Greek and Latin support polite formations expressing a wish that verges on a command.

Such polite subjunctives are also among the possible ways of handling negative commands in Latin as well:

> Ne metuas . . .
>
> *Lest you fear . . .*
>
> *(I.e., Fear not . . .)*
>
> —Martial, *Epigrams* 1.70.13

It is not, however, the only way to handle negative commands. A completely different set of constructions comes into play for these—often distinguished from positive commands by not being called "commands" at all, but rather "prohibitions." In Latin it is de rigueur to use *noli* or *nolite*—the singular and plural forms of the verb *nolo*, which is the negative of *volo*, "wish." Therefore one is not actually telling someone not to do something, but rather not to *wish* to do it. The usage is so ingrained, however, that it has the full force of a negative imperative:

> Nolite cogere socios.
>
> *Do not compel the allies.*
>
> —Cicero, *Against Verres* 2.1.82

This, interestingly, has an equivalent in English that appears occasionally in early modern usage (charged with Latin as it was). In *A Midsummer Night's Dream,* when Bottom has been transformed and sees that his best course of action is to beat a hasty retreat, Titania crosses him with

> Out of this wood **do not desire to go:**
> Thou shalt remain here, whether thou wilt or no.
>
> —William Shakespeare, *A Midsummer Night's Dream* 3.1

One may also find other similar verbs used in the same way as *noli*, though they tend to be far less common.

A final variant but relatively normal form for prohibition is *cave*, "beware," used with the bare subjunctive (not, as one might otherwise expect, with *ne*):

> Cave putes . . .
>
> *Take care lest you think . . .*
>
> *(I.e., Don't think . . . )*
>
> —Cicero, *To Atticus* 7.20

An imperative with a simple negation particle *ne* is not unheard of, but it's chiefly poetic, and virtually never found in prose:

> Equo ne credite, Teucri.
>
> *Do not trust [in] the horse, Trojans.*
>
> —Vergil, *Aeneid* 2.48

Greek, always the language of irregularities, of course has several different ways to do this, depending on the tense and person of the verb being used. To convey a simple "don't do . . ." idea, one normally would use the negation particle μή followed by an aorist subjunctive. To convey a progressive "don't be doing . . ." idea (often equivalent to "stop doing . . ."), one would typically express the prohibition with μή followed either by the present subjunctive (the hortatory use) if the verb is in the first person, or by the present imperative for the second or third person. The key to remembering this is to recall that the present tense is, as noted earlier, part of the imperfect system, and hence expresses generally continuing aspect, especially in moods other than the indicative.

### Infinitive: Not quite a mood

We now come to a cluster of forms—the infinitive, gerund, and participle—that are regular outgrowths of the verb systems, but do not *function* as verbs at all. They are *constructed* from verbs, and they are sometimes treated generically as moods of the verb, but they are not finite moods. They exhibit many of the behaviors of verbs (like the capacity to take objects), but in their operation, they are strictly nouns and adjectives. Most importantly, they cannot express a complete predication on their own.

In English we form the infinitive by taking a neutral form of the verb and tacking the word "to" onto it (not in this case a preposition, but a part of the verb). This is a Germanic idiosyncrasy that survives into modern English: neither Greek nor Latin, nor any of the other languages derived from Latin, has a compound infinitive.

The infinitive functions as a noun if one views it objectively. In the simple sentence

I like to fish.

the infinitive "to fish" is the noun standing as the object of the verb "I like." Consider:

I like computers.
I like cake.
I like to fish.

In such situations, one can also construe the infinitive as being in a special relationship with another verb, where those verbs are sometimes called *auxiliary* or *helping* verbs. It's less a matter of which is right, and more of how you choose to view it. The infinitive of this pair is called the *complementary* infinitive. Note the spelling: it's not a *complimentary* infinitive, which would be a free one, or perhaps one that showered the recipient with praise, but *complementary*—that is, it *completes* the sense of the actual finite verb.

The infinitive *does* retain from its origins the peculiar feature that it supports distinctions in tense:

I want to become wealthy.

versus

I want to have become wealthy.

Because the infinitives in Latin and Greek are normally single words, they are able to be used more flexibly and nimbly than the composite infinitives of English. In certain constructions, too, they do take a kind of pseudosubject, if it is relevant; this will almost invariably be in the accusative case.

## Gerund: The other side of the infinitive

In English we also have another kind of verbal noun called the *gerund*. In many respects it's like the infinitive. It's a verbal noun, though it resembles the English participle in its formation: "swimming" versus "to swim." The English gerund mostly duplicates the function of the infinitive in the subjective and objective cases. We can say:

> To swim across the English Channel is difficult.

or

> Swimming across the English Channel is difficult.

That's using the infinitive and the gerund as the subject; we can easily use either as a direct object as well:

> I like to swim.

or

> I like swimming.

When we need a verbal noun as an object of a preposition, on the other hand, we definitely prefer the gerund, perhaps because following a preposition with the English "to" (which is also, in other contexts, a preposition) sounds bizarre. It would be normal to say:

> It is difficult to cross the English Channel by swimming.

We would be much less likely to say:

> It is difficult to cross the English Channel by to swim.

As we'll see, however, Greek has no problem with this at all.

## Gerunds and infinitives in English, Latin, and Greek

English, Latin, and Greek all deal with gerunds and infinitives differently. We have seen that the English gerund and infinitive tend to overlap, though incompletely: either can be used in some situations, while others require only one.

In Latin, the rules of the game are somewhat different. While Latin does support the complementary infinitive (as does Greek) after certain verbs, in the main, the free use of the infinitive is restricted to the nominative case only. Hence:

> Laborare est orare.
>
> *To work is to pray.*

In all the other cases, Latin will resort to the gerund. The gerund will work *only* in those other cases as well. There is no distinction of number in the Latin gerund, and there is no nominative form either, so one has only the genitive, dative, accusative, and ablative cases in the singular; the gerund endings are *-ndi, -ndo, -ndum, -ndo*. That is all. The Latin gerund is treated as a neuter noun in most respects, though it is typically modified not by an adjective, but by an adverb (a concession to its verbal nature).

In English we can do either. We can say:

> Good speaking requires practice.

or

> Speaking well requires practice.

There is almost no difference in meaning between the two, though one of them emphasizes the static noun-like quality of the gerund, while the other emphasizes the gerund's verbal origin, and the meanings may differ markedly with context:

> I enjoy cooking well.

or

> I enjoy good cooking.

Again, the difference is fairly slight, though the former suggests that one enjoys the activity, whereas the latter implies rather that one enjoys the results of good cooking, wherever they may come from.

Greek simplifies the picture enormously: it has no gerund. As if in compensation, however, it deploys its infinitives in every case. It does this by an expedient not available to Latin, using the article (which Latin lacks completely). One can place a definite article (equivalent to our "the") before any infinitive. Unlike English "the," however, the Greek article is fully inflected for all four of its main cases—nominative, genitive, dative, and accusative. (The article is also inflected for gender and number, but this is immaterial here, since the infinitive is always treated as a neuter singular noun.) The resultant construction is simple and elegant, allowing maximum flexibility. This so-called *articular infinitive* may be used as the subject of a sentence, as the object of a verb, or in any of the oblique cases. Even in this position it can still take an object as well:

> χαλεπὸν τὸ τοῦτο ποιεῖν.
>
> *The to do this is difficult.*
>
> *(I.e., Doing this is difficult.)*

or

> μανθάνομεν τῷ ποιεῖν
>
> *We learn by means of to do.*
>
> *(I.e., We learn by doing.)*

Once you get used to it, the articular infinitive is remarkably powerful and eco-nomical, but a native speaker of English, or someone who has studied only Latin, needs to be sensitive to the fact that it frames ideas in a way that does not corre-spond directly with any English or Latin form of expression.

### Participle: Also not quite a mood

Finally, a verb may be rendered into an adjective. These are called participles, and they are used, one way or another, to modify nouns. In English they are fairly limited. Latin has a somewhat larger range of options. Greek has vastly more. The whole matter is too large to fold in here, so it's discussed more extensively in chapter 9.

# Voice

"Voice" is the peculiar grammatical term used to distinguish the place of the agent in the sentence. If you first learned about it in English, you probably have taken it for granted that there are two possible options—the active and the passive.

It makes a certain amount of sense: in an active sentence, the *subject* is the one acting. In a passive sentence, the subject is the *recipient* of the action—that is, the person or thing being acted upon. Greek also supports a third voice, however, known as the *middle*. Let's take these up in turn.

### Active

The active voice is the obvious one: the subject is the agent—that is, the one performing the action. There's not much to say about it beyond that, insofar as it's active. But it does support another distinction that is the foundation of the other voices, and that is the idea of *transitivity*. We can talk about a verb (and implicitly the action it names) as being *transitive* or *intransitive*; what's being discussed here is the capacity of the action to take an *object*. Two brief examples should suffice:

> Roger walked around the block.
> Babe Ruth hit the baseball.

There is no object for "walk." Walking isn't happening *to* anything or anyone external to the agent—that is, the person doing the walking. The phrase "around the block" modifies the walking adverbially, but it's not an object. We normally consider this kind of verb *intransitive*. (The formulation "walk the dog" is derivative, and is arguably a different sense of the verb altogether. So is the technical baseball use of "walk" for what a pitcher does to a batter by throwing enough balls.)

By contrast, the baseball is actually on the receiving end of the hitting, and so we talk about it as being the *object* of the verb. We have a sense that the action of hitting in some metaphorical sense *passes over* or *crosses over* (Latin *transit*) from the batter to the ball.

As viscerally fundamental as it might seem, however, the notion of transitivity is apparently not as basic a concept as one might intuitively suppose. In fact, it is historically fairly late to appear on the scene. The use of the accusative case to express a direct object, at least in Greek and Latin, appears to be an outgrowth of its more fundamental nature, expressing motion toward or at something. We will return to this in the discussion of the cases. The very concept of transitivity seems therefore to be derivative of the idea of physical movement. Without that concept, however, one could not have the passive voice.

### Passive

The passive voice is much reviled in English composition classes nowadays, and it's certainly true that it is overused, especially in certain kinds of writing. But it has a legitimate place, and pretending that it's not there, or that any appearance of the passive verb is a grammatical error (as some composition instructors claim), is a triumph of the doctrinaire over good sense.

The passive voice is specifically the promotion of the *object* of a transitive verb to the status of the grammatical *subject* of the sentence:

> The Persians were defeated at Marathon.

Accordingly, one cannot really have a passive version of an intransitive sentence—

that is, a sentence that doesn't contain a transitive verb. Without an object, there's nothing to promote.

By displacing the original agent—that is, the subject—the passive removes any account of agency from the basic subject-object relationship of the sentence. Therein lies its beauty and its diabolical slipperiness. The passive voice is a handy way of avoiding responsibility. Politicians, accordingly, are very fond of it:

> Mistakes were made.

Sure they were, but who made them? Some people apparently believe that the passive voice creates a sense of greater objectivity. Most police reports are in the passive voice:

> The subject was apprehended leaving the store with stolen
> merchandise.

The objectivity, of course, is illusory. It's no more objective than any other way of putting it. Some social sciences, too, cultivate a style that entirely eschews active verbs. Again, it's a matter of fostering an impression, rather than achieving the reality, of objectivity.

Still we want to know who's to blame: accordingly, one can reintroduce the agent to such a sentence, and doing so may well be important:

> This baseball was hit by Babe Ruth.
> The Persians were defeated by the allied Greek forces at Marathon.

But the agent construction is a separate one, not apparently fundamental to the subject-object relationship of the sentence any longer. I believe a strong case can be made for the idea that it too derives from the idea of motion—but in this case motion *from*. We'll talk about that specifically in the next chapter when we get to cases and their functions.

It's probably worth pointing out here that there are two profoundly different ways of constructing passive verbs (and accordingly passive sentences), and how one forms them will have a lot to do with how one experiences them as well. The first is with genuinely passive forms of the verb, which is (for the most part) what happens with Greek and Latin. These are sometimes trivially longer than their active counterparts, but usually not by much.

English, on the other hand (and parts of Latin, together with some of the more remote corners of Greek), relies on a *periphrastic* passive—which is to say that it's pieced together with a combination of words, usually involving some form of the verb "to be." Hence to go from

>Babe Ruth hit this baseball.

to

>This baseball was hit by Babe Ruth.

or from

>Babe Ruth will break the bat.

to

>The bat will be broken by Babe Ruth.

one has to introduce "was" or "will be" into the picture. The only way we can convey the passive idea is to use a passive participle. Sometimes that is distinct from other forms of the verb (as in the case of "broken"); sometimes it's not (as in the case of "hit"). Especially if there's no difference in the form, it's the placement of the verb of being that does the trick.

This is certainly one of the reasons passive verbs are so widely disparaged by modern English stylists: they're inflationary. Using a passive verb in a sentence will almost always result in a longer sentence. While there are occasionally other good reasons for using it, most of the time it seems like a poor bargain when the only benefit from the process is the removal of agency (and implicitly responsibility) from the equation.

The same is not quite the case with Latin or Greek, however. In most situations, verbs have passive forms of their own that are not composite. We can say in Latin:

>Ciceronem laudat.

>*[He/she] praises Cicero.*

From there we can go to the almost equally compact

>Cicero laudatur.

>*Cicero is [being] praised.*

Accordingly, the Greeks and Romans didn't employ the passive for the sake of pure verbosity. They still realized, however, that it was a very useful way of dodging responsibility.

## Middle

Beginning students of Greek are often nonplussed to discover that it supports a third voice. The dual number seems unnecessary, but it has a clearly defined rationale; the aorist tense is unfamiliar, but it actually creates an important distinction in aspect. But what, students typically wonder, could possibly be added to the active and passive? Those two seem to provide an exhaustive list of options.

To some extent, they're right. But there's a third voice all the same. The Greek *middle* (occasionally hinted at in Latin, too—especially by poets of a Hellenizing bent) is an odd catchall sort of voice, used to create nuances of meaning not typically supported otherwise. It's not *systematically* used for one thing or another. Instead its usage varies with the particular verb in question. There is, therefore, no simple way of summing up the meaning of the middle, as one can (fairly easily) with the active and the passive.

Nevertheless, one can point out a few places where the middle *tends* to be used. It is used for fundamentally intransitive verbs, or for intransitive applications of verbs that can be both transitive and intransitive. It also can form what looks something like a closed reflexive system, implying that the subject is acting on itself, or for the benefit or advantage of itself.

A few examples will have to suffice. The Greek verb παύω, for example, means "stop." In the active voice, it will tend to mean "stop" in a transitive sense:

> Themistocles stopped me.

In the passive, we can see the obvious converse of that relationship:

> I was stopped by Themistocles.

In the middle, though, the intransitive sense comes to the fore. One could also see it as a form of reflexive; its object is internal, at best:

> Themistocles stopped.

All of those are valid understandings of the term, and the middle voice helps clarify which one is being used at the time.

With a different verb, though, the story may be different. The verb παιδεύω means "educate." The first-person singular active, predictably, means "I teach," while the first-person singular passive just as predictably means "I am taught." So far so good. The middle voice of this particular verb, however, usually refers to *having* someone educated—causing it to happen, in other words, while not doing the actual instruction oneself. I think it is fair to say that nobody is likely to stumble across this meaning intuitively. At the same time, it makes a certain amount of sense eventually, especially in the social and cultural context of classical Athens, and posits an important distinction in the various uses of the word.

All of this may foster an impression of something that is wholly chaotic. Seen from the outside, it may be. But over time, one can develop an impression of how the middle voice is used, and a certain inner logic begins to emerge from it. That we can't really express that logic easily in English is probably partly because there is no equivalent English concept. But forming such concepts is part of the point of learning another language.

### Phantoms: Deponents and semi-deponents

Deponents and semi-deponents are really more a morphological curiosity than anything to do with syntax, so we won't linger on them, but the phenomenon is such that it at least suggests some kind of archaic semantic linkage. Both Greek and Latin have verbs that are passive (or middle, in the case of some Greek verbs) in *form*, while being active in meaning. These are known as *deponents* and *semi-deponents*. Some of them are systematically inverted throughout; others are not. Like the nuances of meaning in the Greek middle, these need to be learned on a case-by-case basis.

# CHAPTER 8

# Nouns—Substantives and Adjectives

*What's in a name*

*Substantives* (what English usually calls nouns) and *adjectives* are, as we discussed in chapter 1, two different kinds of *names* in the broadest ancient understanding of the term. Ancient grammarians tended to distinguish between the *nomen substantivum* and the *nomen adiectivum*. Pronouns offer a few extra wrinkles, and we'll talk about their peculiarities in due course, but a lot of what needs to be said about them falls squarely within a general discussion of nouns and adjectives. They take their places in syntactical constructions in virtually identical ways.

## What names are marked for

We introduced the concept of *marking* for verbs above. This is just a broad, generic way of talking about what kinds of formal flags words carry indicating different facets of their meaning. Verbs, you will recall, are marked for *person, number, tense, mood,* and *voice.* Nouns are marked for three things, again, in a conventional order:

1. Case

2. Number

3. Gender

These are, in a sense, listed in order of decreasing importance, so we'll take them in reverse order.

### Gender

Gender in nouns is almost arbitrary. Grammatical gender is a projection of real-world sex onto things that may or may not actually have sex. One can debate in the airiest abstract terms about whether there is something intrinsically masculine or feminine about the words that are so marked in Latin or Greek; it's unlikely, however, that one will ever be able to arrive at a demonstrable conclusion. The concept seems vaguely puzzling or arbitrary to most speakers of English, since we don't mark our nouns for gender (though we still do have gender differentiation in some of our pronouns—e.g., "he," "she," and "it"). What *is* clear, however, is that linguistic morphology trumps nature: a certain form of a noun may be characteristically masculine, feminine, or neuter, and it will retain that form, even if being applied to something of a different real-world sex. Beginning students of German (especially English speakers) are often amused by the fact that *das Mädchen* (the girl) is a neuter noun. But it's a neuter *not* because of some gender confusion on the part of either the speaker or the girl, but because *any* noun with the diminutive suffix *-chen* is neuter. It's a diminutive of *die Magd* (the maid, woman), which is (unsurprisingly) feminine. Latin *virtus* ("virtue, courage": strictly, "manliness," from *vir*, "man") is feminine. This is not because it's seen as a feminine attribute of men, but because nouns ending in *-tus, -tutis* are always feminine. In fact, almost all Latin abstract nouns (those ending in *-tus, -tutis; -tas, -tatis; -tudo, -tudinis,* etc.) are feminine. Can we say that the Romans considered abstraction somehow feminine? It seems unlikely, but perhaps cannot be ruled out entirely.

There are exceptions. The first-declension nouns in Latin are virtually all feminine, and the adjectives built on the same model are invariably feminine. But there are a few first-declension nouns—mostly involving one's line of work, and mostly derivative of Greek—that are in fact masculine. They include the common *agricola* (farmer), *nauta* (sailor), *poeta* (poet), *pirata* (pirate), and a few others. They are *understood* to be masculine, irrespective of the morphological clues, and if you want to modify such a noun with an adjective, you need to pick a masculine form. A good farmer is not an *agricola bona* but an *agricola bonus*. In the same way, second-declension nouns ending with *-us* are typically masculine; but the names of plants—*quercus* (oak), *pinus* (pine), *fraxinus* (ash), and so on—as well as the names of gems, countries, and towns ending in *-us*, and a few other odd words, are in fact feminine. What does one make of this? Language is a quirky real-world phenomenon. Even the ever-so-regular Latin is subject to exceptions. As for Greek . . . it's virtually made of exceptions.

## Number

Number is intrinsic to whatever you're talking about at the moment: is there just one duck or are there several or many? In very early Latin, as in early Greek and even early forms of Old English, there is a dual. Most of the time, we don't need to pay it very much heed. The dual tends to crop up in nouns about as frequently as it crops up in verbs—they go together.

There are a few minor wrinkles in number. Typically these occur at the crossroads of number—collectives and distributives. British and American English, for example, diverge on collective nouns. Americans base grammatical agreement on strict morphology, viewing the collective as a single entity, whereas the British refer to the referent as if to its constitutent members. An American would say:

The State Department has banned travel to these countries.

A Briton would say instead:

The Foreign Office have banned travel to these countries.

Latin does something similar, though in a different way. Occasionally one gets a *distributive* sense of a noun, in which a single feature or attribute is mapped to multiple entities. There, it will normally retain a singular form in Latin; for example,

Ex ore infantium

*Out of the mouth of babes*

We would normally say:

Out of the mouths of babes

Mass nouns and discrete units offer unique problems in every language. Good English writers tend to make a clear distinction between them, but other languages draw the lines in different places. One occasionally hears in colloquial English something like this:

If we raise the ticket prices, less people will come.

"Less," however, (unlike its counterpart "more") is normally reserved for mass nouns:

For a drier mixture, use less water.
Construction in this way will require less concrete.

The proper form of the first sentence in standard modern English would be the following:

If we raise the ticket prices, **fewer** people will come.

Reducing people to the status of mass nouns is seen as dehumanizing—though one may occasionally see it done deliberately, with an eye to viewing them as an undifferentiated mass, as Vergil does:

> . . . rumpunt aditus primosque trucidant
> immissi Danai et late loca milite complent.
>
> *. . . they break down the door, and the Greeks having gained access*
> *slaughter the first ones, and fill the whole place with soldier.*

—Vergil, *Aeneid* 2.494–95

The effect is chilling. Translators shy away from such a blunt statement in English: one will occasionally see it rendered as "soldiery" or the like, but Vergil's intention is fairly clear. He wants us to see the Greek soldiers as a mass of undifferentiated and impersonal hatred, as faceless as the masked storm troopers of *Star Wars*.

Similarly, Latin uses *pars* (part, some) in places where we'd never use the cognate "part"; again, that is reserved for mass nouns—"part of the flour" but never "part of the flowers." But this is probably chiefly a matter of lexical domains that have shifted over time.

## Case

The big determinant in the syntax of nouns is *case*. Our grammatical term "case" comes from Latin *casus*, which means "falling"; it in turn is borrowed as a concept from the Greek πτῶσις (*ptōsis*, which also means "falling"). However one understands it, it expresses the way the word falls in the sentence or clause—its position or placement in the syntactic structure. In general, that's reflected in both Latin and Greek by the endings of nouns. There are other ways to achieve the same effect, however, and languages are constantly evolving in this regard. Old English has a range of grammatical cases not much different from those of modern German; modern English has very largely lost them, retaining only two really distinctive grammatical cases—a subjective and an objective case. Those are functional, rather than morphological distinctions: they show up in the forms of our pronouns, but no longer in our nouns at all. In the sentences

> I hit him.
> He hit me.

the forms of the subject and object are distinct. In other sentences, however, such as

> Tom hit the baseball.
> The baseball hit Tom.

the only thing determining the subject-object relationship is word order. In Latin and Greek, it is much different. Most of the rest of this chapter will be about the constructions that can be made with the various cases.

Here we can get an enormous amount of leverage once again from looking back at the structures of Proto-Indo-European. Proto-Indo-European had a large number of cases. Latin and Greek draw their case structures from this rich set, but each language reduces the number of cases, combining a few of the originals into a single case. Unsurprisingly, they don't do this in precisely the same way. This can cause considerable confusion for those first learning Latin and Greek—but it can also provide a way out of the confusion. The relationship between how those cases collapsed in each language can shed some light on where individual *uses* of the cases in various constructions came from.

## English cases

English retains, as should be apparent by now, only a very simplified case structure, reduced (chiefly through the influence of French) from a fairly full Germanic set of cases in Old English to two—a subjective case (used for the subject of the verb or for the predicate nominative) and an objective case (used for everything else—the object of the verb or a preposition). In most cases, even this is a purely analytical distinction, since English nouns are not themselves inflected in any way. The distinction in form survives exclusively in pronouns (*I, me; he, him; she, her; we, us; they, them; who, whom; etc.*). This simplified system does not of course prevent an outrageous number of case errors from occurring in English all the same, from the illiterate formation

Me and Tom went to the ocean.

to the hypercorrect form (that is, an error made as a reaction to a mistakenly perceived error in the proper form)

Please discuss this afterward with Sally and I.

Such errors occur chiefly in compound subjects or objects: no native speaker would say:

Me went to the ocean.

or

Please discuss this afterward with I.

Remembering to use the same form as one would use in an uncompounded subject or object is probably the simplest way to avoid errors in this remarkably simple case system.

## Cases in Greek, Latin, and PIE

The cases of Greek and Latin ultimately go back to the eight Proto-Indo-European cases shown in figure 7. As the languages evolved, there was a tendency for multiple cases to coalesce or collapse into one; this did not, however, always happen in the same way. The chart shows that the Latin ablative expresses an original ablative and an original instrumental; the Greek genitive, on the other hand, represents the Proto-Indo-European ablative together with its genitive, while the instrumental has fallen in with the Greek dative. With this fairly small amount of information, we can draw some interesting (though perhaps somewhat provisional) conclusions about the sources and even the underlying thinking behind a number of constructions.

It must be said that almost any description of the cases and their main functions is approximate and somewhat reductive: as languages grow and develop, forms that are already available take on new functions at need, as outgrowths of earlier ones, expanding and stretching in novel and occasionally bewildering ways. Nevertheless, I'll try to give a general summary of the cases and their meanings,

**Fig. 7.** Greek, Latin, and Proto-Indo-European Cases

| Latin | Proto-Indo-European | Greek |
|---|---|---|
| nominative | nominative (subject) | nominative |
| genitive | genitive (possession, belonging) | genitive |
| ablative | ablative (motion from, separation) | genitive |
| ablative | instrumental (means) | dative |
| dative | dative (reference, association) | dative |
| accusative | accusative (motion toward) | accusative |
| vocative | vocative (direct address) | vocative |
| locative | locative (place where) | locative |

and then follow up with a closer analysis of the particular constructions.

## Nominative

The nominative case is the naming case. It is used almost exclusively either for the subject of a sentence or clause, or for something modifying the subject directly. It's the least variable of all the cases, and it is the basic form one looks up in a lexicon. In Greek and Latin, the nominative form is typically not sufficient to provide one with enough information to create all inflected forms, and hence the nominative normally needs to be learned along with the genitive form and the gender. In Latin, the gender is an independent fact; in Greek one can learn the gender as embodied in the article.

The two main functions of the nominative, therefore, are to provide the subject for a clause (or to modify it attributively), and to provide predicate nominatives after a copulative use of the verb of being. Predicate nominatives (broadly classified) fall into two subcategories—predicate nouns (or substantives, to adhere to ancient terminology) and predicate adjectives. The predicate adjective will always agree with the subject in number and gender as well as in case. Predicate substantives have their own number and gender, unrelated to the number and gender of the subject:

> The dead fish on the sidewalk are a mess.

One would be hard put to know how else one could manage such a situation, since in equating one noun with another one must inevitably (at least some of the time) wind up pairing things where the number or the gender is not the same.

There are cases (especially in Latin and Greek) in which a predicate adjective modifies an *understood* predicate noun, not expressed, as in the Vergilian dictum

> Varium et mutabile semper femina.
>
> —Vergil, *Aeneid* 4.449

By any normal construction, one would expect:

> Varia et mutabilis semper femina.
>
> *A woman is always variable and changeable.*

but the implication of Vergil's line is rather

> A woman is always a variable and changeable [thing].

Hence the neuter adjectives express the understood "thingness" of the predicate nominative. This may seem all the more peculiar to an English speaker, since if the word "thing" were actually expressed, it would be the feminine *res*. But this is not the thought pattern implicit in the statement. Aside from this kind of issue, however, there are very few surprises with the nominative case.

## Genitive

With the genitive case, things begin to get interesting. The genitive case is normally understood as the case of possession—translated typically with the English preposition "of." But this is somewhat too weak an understanding to account for its many, varied uses. Greek is further complicated by the fact that its genitive case represents not only the Proto-Indo-European genitive case, but also its *ablative* case (see figure 7).

The genitive basically turns the noun in question into something like an adjective: that is, it *modifies* a noun just as an adjective would, and one can use a genitive noun almost anywhere one could otherwise use another kind of adjective, in English, Greek, or Latin:

> the blue book
> Tom's book
> (i.e., the of-Tom book)

In Greek, where attributive adjectives (i.e., nonpredicate adjectives) are routinely tucked in between the article and its noun, the genitive is inserted in exactly the same way. For Latin, of course, no such rule obtains, since Latin has no article, but the adjectival function remains all the same.

In Greek, Latin, and English alike, the genitives run alongside a set of possessive adjectives (or adjectival pronouns). For English-speaking students, these may initially create some confusion in idiom, but this is something more likely to crop up in composition than in reading and understanding texts. The meaning is unaltered: it merely happens that each language has its own rules for which kind of word should be preferred in any given instance. In Latin, where a possessive adjective is available, it should usually be used in preference to the genitive of the personal pronoun; in Greek, that's not always the case.

## Ablative

The fundamental idea behind the ablative is *separation* or *motion from*—what we might call "from-ness." In this respect it forms a reciprocal pair with the accusative, which expresses *motion toward*—"to-ness" or "at-ness," if you like. The ablative is, however, dominated chiefly by an underlying idea of *motion*. In loose English usage, it may seem to overlap significantly the domain of the genitive, since in such phrases as these:

Dionysius of Halicarnassus

Κυναίγειρος ὁ Εὐφορίωνος

*Kynaigeiros the [son] of Euphorion*

the underlying concept seems to be one of origin (either city or family). But arguably the genitive that appears there refers more to *belonging* than to *coming from* somewhere in particular.

Students are often confounded by the Latin ablative because it presents so many different and seemingly arbitrary faces, but this is largely because it is a conflation of two Proto-Indo-European cases—the true ablative and the instrumental. If one sorts the ablative constructions into these two classes, they are much easier to grasp. This also goes a long way toward explaining why a number of apparently very similar constructions emerge in different cases in Latin and Greek.

The motion-based idea of the ablative is easily transferred to other more metaphorical understandings of motion, and I will argue below that this is an important piece of understanding how agent constructions (among others) work in both Latin and Greek. But it's a good idea to keep the physical referent in mind at the outset, since the figurative use of a case seldom strays very far from its literal sense.

Complicating these matters for students of Greek is the fact that there is no ablative case as such: its functions have fallen in with the genitive case. We will discuss strategies for keeping these distinct shortly.

## Instrumental and associative

The Proto-Indo-European instrumental case appears in some of the early Germanic languages (including Old English), but in both Greek and Latin it has been assimilated to another case. This causes considerable confusion among students learning elementary Greek or Latin, but it need not. In Greek the instrumental has fallen in with the dative case; in Latin it has fallen in with the ablative. Keeping the functions separate, however, is a relatively easy matter once one comes to see how the different constructions are employed and what their underlying ideas are.

The fundamental notion of the instrumental case is "with-ness"—it expresses the means or instrumentality by which something is done. Thus it applies normally to impersonal means, not to persons. People are more usually viewed as agents, unless they are seen merely as means to an end, subordinate to another agency. Hence one might say:

He broke the gate with an axe.
Alexander conquered Persia with [by means of] an enormous army.

Some Indo-European languages had an *associative* case distinct from the instrumental. The associative case represents accompaniment ("with" in the sense of being alongside someone or something, rather than "with" in the sense of being a means or instrument):

I went to the store with my credit card. (*accompaniment*)
I bought a pair of shoes with my credit card. (*instrument*)

In many Indo-European languages, though, while the associative and instrumental functions remain meaningfully distinct, they tend to have convergent forms and very similar patterns of use. One can see why: usually the means by which one does something, especially in a practical and physical context, is also accompanying the agent. While I may contact an old friend by means of e-mail, I cannot build a box with a hammer unless I also have the hammer in my possession. The domains of instrumentality and association, therefore, can frequently overlap, and this will prove important in view of some of the specific constructions. We will have occasion to refer (as other grammars sometimes do as well) to an "instrumental-associative case," at least at the theoretical level. There is of course no such case explicitly in either Latin or Greek.

Both of these concepts, however, are quite different in origin and in meaning from the agent construction with passive verbs. We will shortly look at why.

## Dative

The dative case is often explained as the case of the indirect object, and that's not a bad explanation as far as it goes, but the core notion of the dative is more accurately understood as having to do with relationship: "at-ness" or "with-respect-to-ness." The name "dative" derives from the Latin *casus dativus*, which comes from the principal verb of giving, *do, dare*; in Greek it is called ἡ δοτικὴ πτῶσις, which effectively means the same thing. It is not, however, confined to this sense, and its domain takes in almost any kind of idea of respect or relationship. As such, one could see it as forming a kind of antithetical pair with the instrumental, since the instrumental points to the means *by* which something is accomplished, and the dative to the sense or context *for* which it is relevant. Complicating this picture, unfortunately, is the fact that in Greek the instrumental has fallen together with the dative to make a single case, so that the two notions tend to converge, rather than being kept entirely separate. The meanings in question, however, are seldom confusing in context.

Native speakers of English are likely to be too eager to draw "to" into their definitions of the dative; E. C. Woodcock argues that "for" probably conveys the sense of the word much more successfully than "to" does. Almost all the uses of the dative can be thought of in basically relational terms. Almost anything involving actual physical motion toward a goal of any sort is carried by the accusative instead.

In both Greek and Latin, the dative case tends to have many lexically specific applications. There are a number of verbs—particularly compound verbs—that (while they might take a direct object in English) require a dative pseudo-object or indirect object in Latin or Greek.

## Accusative

In elementary Latin and Greek courses, the accusative is normally explained as the case of the direct object—the thing or person to or upon which the action of the main verb is performed. This is somewhat unfortunate, for two reasons. In the first place, transitivity—the capacity of a verb to take a direct object—is apparently a fairly late development in language. As fundamental as it may seem to us, it is, as E. C. Woodcock persuasively argues (*A New Latin Syntax*, §§1–2) , a derivative sense. In the second place, the accusative also supports a number of other meanings that really don't have much connection to the concept of the direct object. It's almost certainly better to understand it primarily in physical terms, as having to do with *motion toward* an object: "to-ness" (in a physical sense, as opposed to the relational one that is the domain of the dative) or "at-ness." From this figure of thought one can reasonably derive an idea of the direct object, and indeed it need not leave that physical image entirely behind. If we take the sentence

Tom hits the baseball.

we can understand that at bottom this means something more like this:

Tom directs his hitting at [in the direction of, toward, to] the baseball.

The accusative is also used for all manner of functions where motion toward a goal is the idea nearest the surface. Latin students beginning from English perennially want to use the dative for such things, but it's not correct.

He came to Athens.

does not employ the dative, but rather the bare accusative:

Athenas venit.

The same is true of Greek.

The accusative is also used for boundary or limit conditions toward which something is moving—hence the accusative of extent of time or space:

> *They marched for three days.*
>
> Tres dies iter fecerunt.
>
> *They marched for four miles.*
>
> Quattuor milia [passuum] iter fecerunt.

Again, Greek retains a virtually identical usage for the accusative. We will explore all these constructions in greater detail below.

### Locative

The locative case is one of the relatively minor cases in both Greek and Latin, and while one needs to know it, its meaning remains blessedly uncomplicated. It conveys the notion of *where* something happened—that's all. It is used relatively infrequently in both Greek and Latin, many of its functions having been quietly taken over by other cases (especially the ablative in Latin) after a preposition like *in*.

### Vocative

The vocative is similarly simple: it is used only for direct address. In some instances the forms are identical with the nominative, but where there is a distinct form, it is reliably used. In Latin one would never address Marcus as *Marcus*, but rather as *Marce*. Simplifying this further is the fact that the vocative does not participate in any syntactically complex functions: a vocative word or phrase is normally tacked on to another clause or sentence without interfering with the subtler processes of that predication, and so it almost never offers any real difficulty either in recognition or in interpretation.

## The individual constructions

I have taken it as axiomatic here that most if not all of the individual case constructions in Greek and Latin can be understood as outgrowths of basically physical models of thought, extended metaphorically or analogically as needed from the tangible to the intangible, creating matrices of ideas that, even if abstract, still to some extent mirror their more concrete ancestors. I have further proceeded on the assumption that languages tend to be conservative in their treatment of these fundamental structures of meaning—that they will tend to change most slowly of all language features (morphology changing more quickly, and phonetics more quickly still).

Both of those contentions are probably open to dispute, and I doubt that either is rigorously demonstrable. In their defense I can merely say that, on the one hand, they make sense to me as an observer of how my own thought and expression take shape and change, and, on the other, that they seem to correspond to the phenomena that emerge from the study of historical linguistics. I hope that what follows will suffice to affirm that correspondence. On those principles, therefore, I shall try carefully to dissect a number of individual case constructions in Greek and Latin, in order to suggest at least a plausible rationale for how they evolved from common Indo-European ancestors, and how they still carry much of the same semantic burden. Please note: I have made no attempt to be exhaustive here; this is not, after all, a reference grammar in design or conception. My main purpose is to help the student construct an organic conceptual framework strong enough to support and (ideally) assimilate the other constructions as they appear.

The nominative, locative, and vocative cases are sufficiently simple that they really require no further elaboration; what follows primarily focuses on the other cases.

### Place, space, and time

If most of the constructions engaging the oblique cases of the noun are indeed derived from a physical prototype, it probably behooves us, first of all, to nail down the elements of that model as clearly as we can before moving to their more obscure ramifications. The core meanings here, I would contend, are those relating one entity—be it person or thing—to another in spatial terms. At the simplest level, three relationships can obtain: $x$ can be moving toward $y$, $x$ can be stationary with respect to $y$, or $x$ can be moving away from $y$. In the early Indo-European languages, these three states are expressed by the accusative, instrumental/associative, and ablative cases, respectively. Even after a good deal of later development and metaphorical extension, these relationships remain at the core of the three cases.

One can envision all this quite simply as shown in figure 8: the ablative represents the source, and the accusative the goal or limit of any extension or activity; the instrumental (shadowing the locative) and the PIE dative represent location where—"at" in the static sense. From this basic framework, we can spin

**Fig. 8.** Cases and Movement

| PIE Ablative | PIE Instrumental | PIE Accusative |
|:---:|:---:|:---:|
| Gk. **Genitive** | Gk. **Dative** | Gk. **Accusative** |
| Lat. **Ablative** | Lat. **Ablative** | Lat. **Accusative** |
| "from" | "at" | "toward" |

out virtually all of the separate constructions relating to time and space in both Latin and Greek.

### Place

The ablative emerges, as noted, as a genitive in Greek and an ablative in Latin, and the instrumental as an ablative in Latin and a dative in Greek. The accusative remains accusative in both languages. The core concept behind the ablative is motion away from or out of something, while the core concept of the accusative is motion toward something. Stationary presence with respect to something else is generally indicated by the instrumental or associative (sometimes the dative, for a slightly different reason), which finds expression as the dative in Greek or the ablative in Latin.

In historical time, certainly, many of these physical concepts were expressed with the help of reinforcing prepositions, but the fundamental concepts inherent in the cases remained a central factor in their meanings. In other words, I think we can argue that though prepositions will color and shape these uses, and help to make them less ambiguous, they will not typically recast them in a wholly new light.

The *place from which* construction, therefore, presents the PIE ablatival idea at something close to its essential nature. Static distance from something is often expressed using ablatival structures as well, as if distance had been accomplished at some point by an act of removal, whether that was in fact the case or not. This should not be surprising, since in English we also talk about one thing being far *from* another, whether they originated in the same place or not. The bare genitive or ablative may occur in especially older poetic usage; more commonly in prose it will be accompanied by a preposition:

> Οὐλύμποιο κατήλθομεν
>
> *We came down from Olympus*
>
> —Homer, *Iliad* 20.125

> negotiator ex Africa
>
> *a merchant from Africa*
>
> —Cicero, *Against Verres* 2.1.14

The *place where* construction is often (not unreasonably) considered an outgrowth of the locative, but I have not found any grammar that could offer any good reasons for *why* this lateral movement should take place. I think it can more easily be understood in light of the basic associative idea that often travels with the instrumental. It predictably emerges as an ablative in Latin and as a dative in Greek. Again, the bare formation is well attested in poetry, while prepositions will more frequently appear with it in prose, though there are a few exceptions:

> τόξ᾽ ὤμοισιν ἔχων
>
> *having a bow on his shoulders*
>
> —Homer, *Iliad* 1.45

> si in Gallia remanerent
>
> *if they remained in Gaul*
>
> —Caesar, *Gallic War* 4.8

The accusative of *place to which* represents motion toward something in two ways—either with the bare accusative (usually reserved for towns and small islands) or with the accusative prepared with a preposition (in Latin usually *ad*, and also usually implying something about the region, rather than the specific location). Again, it expresses the fundamental idea of motion toward:

> Ἀνέβη μέγαν οὐρανὸν Οὔλυμπόν τε.
>
> *She ascended to the broad heaven and to Olympus.*
>
> —Homer, *Iliad* 1.497

> nimborum in patriam, loca feta furentibus Austris,
> Aeoliam venit.
>
> *Into the homeland of the clouds, a place full of raging winds,*
> *to Aeolia she came.*
>
> —Vergil, *Aeneid* 1.51–52

and also (with the more common preposition in prose)

> ad Alesiam perveniunt
>
> *they come to [the region of] Alesia*
>
> —Caesar, *Gallic War* 7.45

### Personal source

The ablative of *personal source* is obviously an outgrowth of the original separative idea, and it (predictably) emerges with a Latin ablative and a Greek genitive form:

> Μάθε μου τάδε.
>
> *Know this of [from] me.*
>
> —Xenophon, *The Education of Cyrus* 1.6

### Space

In the wake of these place relationships between entities or persons, we can form a similar set of constructions relating to *space*—a slightly more rarefied notion, if only because it's made to refer to a more objective frame of reference. Here measurement and quantification come into play, but otherwise the constructions are remarkably similar.

The accusative of *extent of space* represents, therefore, the endpoint—and hence the goal or target—of the motion or extent of space in question, viewed as a quantitative, rather than a concrete, endpoint. It thus preserves the primordial sense of the accusative as an expression of motion *toward* something, while adapting it to a more abstract context. Allen and Greenough's *New Latin Grammar* (§386) classifies the accusative of extent among the "idiomatic uses" of the accusative (seemingly suggesting that they are marginal or peculiar). I would argue that this could hardly be further from the truth: they are very close to the essential nature of the case:

> Ἀπέχει ἡ Πλάταια τῶν Θηβῶν **σταδίους ἑβδομήκοντα**
>
> *Plataea is seventy stades from Thebes*
>
> —Thucydides, *Peloponnesian War*, 2.5

> progressus **milia passuum circiter duodecim**
>
> *having advanced about twelve miles*
>
> —Caesar, *Gallic War* 7.72

On the same principles we can rationalize the concept of space within which, or space where, though neither in pure form is very common. Both do, however, have a closely following analogue in the area of time constructions.

### Time

To arrive at the constructions reflecting time, we need do no more than imagine time as a metaphorically linear extension analogous to extension in space—

virtually all the attendant constructions fall into place with perfect symmetry.

The accusative of *extent of time* represents the goal or target of the motion or extent through time:

αἱ σπονδαὶ **ἐνιαυτὸν** ἔσονται

*the treaty will be for one year*

—Thucydides, *Peloponnesian War* 4.118

cum **triduum** iter fecisset

*when he had marched [for] three days.*

—Caesar, *Gallic War* 7.24

*Time when* similarly follows the instrumental-associative pathway, giving us a Greek dative and a Latin ablative:

**δεκάτῳ ἔτει** ξυνέβησαν

*they reached an accord in the tenth year*

—Thucydides, *Peloponnesian War* 1.103

Quae fuerit **hesterno die** Cn. Pompei gravitas in dicendo, iudices, quae facultas, quae copia, non opinione tacita vestrorum animorum, sed perspicua admiratione declarari videbatur.

*How great was the energy displayed by Cnaeus Pompeius in speaking yesterday, O judges, how great his fluency, how great the riches of his eloquence, was shown plainly enough, not only by the secret feelings of your minds, but by your evident and unconcealed admiration.*

—Cicero, *For Balbus* 2; trans. C. D. Yonge

The only even slightly odd player in this mixture is the construction of *time within which*. Most Latin grammars in fact normally group this with *time when*— many merely referring to a single construction, the *ablative of time when or within which*. The two do certainly coincide in Latin as an ablative, but in Greek, time within which is not framed as a dative (as is the *time when* construction) but as a genitive. Allen and Greenough ascribe it to a locative function of the ablative (§423), but I believe there is good reason to think that these are in origin not the same thing at all, and they are easier to understand holistically if one separates them. The Latin *ablative of time within which* is both more coherent and easier to square with its Greek counterpart if one conceives of it as a *time from which*—that is, out of which extent of time—the events emerge:

Δέκα ἐτῶν οὐκ ἥξουσι.

*They will not come within ten years.*

—Plato, *Laws* 642e

**Diebus viginti quinque** aggerem exstruxerunt.

*Within twenty-five days they finished constructing the mound.*

—Caesar, *Gallic War* 7.24

Note that all three of these time and space constructions are in an important sense adverbial, and not to be confused with the adjectival *genitive of measure*, which remains genitive in both Greek and Latin. The genitive virtually always takes an adjectival direction:

ὀκτὼ σταδίων τεῖχος

*a wall of eight stades*

fossa **trium pedum**

*a ditch of three feet*

## Comparison

*Comparison* can be accomplished in Greek and Latin in two distinct ways. The most secure and probably the most comfortable method of comparison for English speakers is to set up a comparative conjunction meaning "than"—Greek ἤ or Latin *quam*—followed by a noun in the same case as the one being compared.

Where confusion won't result from the compression, however (and sometimes where it will), the thing compared is often expressed without a "than," using an ablatival construction—which is to say that it emerges by way of a Latin ablative or a Greek genitive:

He is taller **than I** [i.e., "of me" or "from me"].

. . . θᾶττον γὰρ **θανάτου** θεῖ.

*for it [wickedness] runs faster than death.*

—Plato, *Apology* 39b

Vilius argentum est **auro, virtutibus** aurum.

*Silver is less valuable than gold, and gold [is less valuable] than virtue.*

—Horace, *Epistles* 1.1.52

Clearly this is in origin an ablatival (separative) concept: he is taller *from* me—that is, in separation from or in distinction to—me. Viewed this way, the constructions in both Greek and Latin converge and seem less arbitrary and confusing.

## Instrumentality

As noted earlier, instrumentality—the means *by which* something is done—was expressed in Proto-Indo-European by its own instrumental case. The instrumental has a long and distinguished history, and even survives into the Germanic languages, including Old English.

Given its obvious utility, what may be surprising is that by historical times—which is to say those times from which we have surviving texts of any length—neither Greek nor Latin has a distinct instrumental case any longer. In both languages, the instrumental case has fallen into another. In Greek it became part of the dative. In Latin it became part of the ablative, and there are Latin *ablative of means* and Greek *dative of means* constructions to prove it. There are a few irregularities about this convergence of the various pieces that become clear in what follows, but they are not enormously problematic, and probably don't require any elaboration here.

## Manner

*Manner* constructions are typically done in Greek with the dative case, but in Latin with the ablative, which puts them squarely in the camp of the other instrumental-associative constructions. It's reasonable to consider manner constructions as being somewhere along the spectrum from means to accompaniment. They describe things that enable, facilitate, or accompany the action, whatever it is, in something more than an incidental way. Take, for example, the following:

> κραυγῇ πολλῇ ἐπίασιν
> *They will advance with a loud shout.*
>
> —Herodotus, *Histories* 6.112

> Magna cum laude
> *With great honor*

In one respect these are similar to *genitives of quality*: most often, they're accompanied by a quantifier, especially in those situations where the characteristic or manner unqualified could be considered normative or obvious, and where the quantity is the main point of information. In these examples, the point is not that there was a shout, but that it was loud, and not that there was some honor, but that there was great honor. In Latin, the word *cum* is necessary if there isn't an accompanying adjective, and optional if there is.

## Objects of verbs, direct and indirect

The *direct object* of a verb is always in the accusative. The direct object refers to what is affected by the action of the transitive verb. As discussed above, this is apparently an outgrowth of the goal-of-motion figure of thought. It is, however, important to remember that not everything we conceive of as being transitive in English is also transitive in Greek or Latin. These curiosities must be learned lexically.

Normally, the direct object will be expressed in the accusative, while the *indirect object*, where one exists, is in the dative:

> I hit the baseball.
>
> I gave the book **to him**.

This will occur frequently after verbs of giving, telling, showing, entrusting, and sometimes other verbs that are felt as having an indirect object—"command," "answer," and so on. In Greek and Latin, as in English, there are usually variant forms for referring to these activities with and without indirect objects:

> Caesar iussit legionem.
>
> *Caesar commanded the legion. (direct object)*
>
> Caesar legioni imperavit.
>
> *Caesar gave orders to the legion. (indirect object)*

The particular constructions required just need to be learned as part of the lexical information about each word.

Similar complications arise between direct objects and means; in English, one might say:

> We threw rocks at the approaching soldiers.

We understand here that the rock is the thing thrown; the approaching soldiers are put into a prepositional phrase, acting adverbially to modify the whole construction. Greek, however, takes a different approach. It's not necessarily any more or less accurate or correct than the English one; but Greek would normally say:

> λίθοις εἰσεβάλλομεν τοὺς στρατιώτας τοὺς ἐπίοντας.

which is to say, effectively:

> *We threw-at the approaching soldiers with [by means of] rocks.*

Note, however, that if we select a slightly different English verb, we wind up with something that works exactly the same way:

> We pelted the approaching soldiers with rocks.

## Objects of prepositions

It is worth recalling at the outset that prepositions are fundamentally adverbs in origin, and a majority of prepositional phrases continue to carry an obviously adverbial burden. The preposition, so analyzed, is merely an adverb that has acquired a conventional relationship to an object of some sort or another, and has become fossilized in this form.

Prepositions in Latin and Greek take objects in the instrumental, the ablative, and the accusative. What this means in practical terms (as you can see in figures 9 and 10) is that Greek prepositions can have objects in the genitive (originally ablative), the dative (originally instrumental), and the accusative. In Latin, these three cases have collapsed into two—the ablative and the accusative.

### *Latin prepositions*

Most Latin prepositions take an accusative object. Of those prepositions in regular and established use, a very short list invariably take the ablative:

| | | |
|---|---|---|
| ab (a) | coram | cum |
| de | ex (e) | prae |
| pro | sine | |

*Tenus, palam, procul, absque,* and *simul* are also sometimes analyzed as prepositions with the ablative, and sometimes as adverbs. One can read Latin for years, however, without encountering some of them at all.

There are only four prepositions that take *both* the accusative and the ablative, and the distinction in their usage is particularly instructive:

| | | |
|---|---|---|
| in | sub | subter |
| super | | |

Where one of these four prepositions is used with an accusative object, its meaning (consistent with the fundamental notion of "toward-ness" or "at-ness") will

**Fig. 9.** Latin Prepositions

| Preposition | Accusative | Ablative | Genitive |
|:---:|:---:|:---:|:---:|
| a, ab | — | from | — |
| ad | to, at | — | — |
| adversus | toward, against | — | — |
| ante | before | — | — |
| apud | by, before | — | — |
| circa | around | — | — |
| circiter | about | — | — |
| circum | around | — | — |
| cis | this side of | — | — |
| citra | this side of | — | — |
| clam | unknown to | — | — |
| coram | — | in the presence of | — |
| contra | against | — | — |
| cum | — | with | — |
| de | — | from, down from | — |
| e, ex | — | from, out of | — |
| erga | toward | — | — |
| extra | outside | — | — |
| in | into (motion) | in (static) | — |
| infra | below | — | — |
| inter | between | — | — |
| intus | — | within | — |
| iuxta | next to, close by | — | — |
| ob | before, on account of | — | — |
| palam | — | in the presence of | — |
| penes | in the power of | — | — |
| per | through | — | — |
| pone | behind | — | — |
| post | behind, following | — | — |
| prae | — | in front of | — |
| praeter | beyond | — | — |
| pro | — | before | — |
| procul | — | far away from | — |
| prope | near, next to | — | — |
| propter | because of | — | — |
| secundum | according to, following | — | — |
| simul | — | together with | — |
| sine | — | without | — |
| sub | under (motion) | under (static) | — |
| subter | under (motion) | under (static) | — |
| super | over (motion) | over (static) | — |
| supra | above, over | — | — |
| tenus | — | as far as | as far as |
| trans | across | — | — |
| ultra | beyond | — | — |
| usque | up to, as far as | — | — |
| versus | toward, against | — | — |

convey *motion into* a situation. Hence *in* with the accusative effectively means the same thing as our "into"; *in* with the ablative (arguably originally an instrumental notion) expresses a state of repose:

> Eunt in casam.
>
> *They are going into the house.*

but

> Sunt in casa.
>
> *They are in the house.*

A completely parallel sense governs the other three, *sub, subter,* and *super.*

In Latin, all other prepositions take the accusative, all the time. A more thorough list of almost everything that can function as a preposition in Latin is provided in figure 9, but it adds relatively little practical information to these handy rules of thumb.

### *Greek prepositions*

The Greek system is somewhat more complicated. Sorting out the Greek prepositions and their objects ultimately requires that you memorize which prepositions take which objects to produce which meanings. Nevertheless, a basic grasp of their clustered meanings will go a long way toward simplifying the apparent chaos.

As one can see from the chart of Greek prepositions (figure 10), all those prepositions that have a fundamental idea of movement *from* (ἀπό, ἐκ, and the relevant senses of παρά and ὑπό) are given to the genitive, which bespeaks an original ablative force. Those that have a basic notion of movement *toward* (ἀνά, εἰς, and the relevant senses of ἐπί, παρά, περί, πρός, ὑπέρ, and ὑπό) take the accusative. The ones that take the dative are generally those in which we find a sense of stasis—"at-ness" in the locative sense, rather than anything involving motion. Most conspicuous among these is of course ἐν, which is contrasted with εἰς much as *in* with the ablative compares to *in* with the accusative in Latin. But the sense of σύν arguably is similar in kind, since it expresses the idea that something is with or by something else, not in motion either toward it or away from it.

A few of the prepositions have what would have to be considered unique meanings for each of the case constructions, and they simply must be learned. There is some correlation with the general system in the case of ἐπί, for example, but it is not quite stable enough to submit to easy analysis this way. The general pattern, however, will help.

**Fig. 10.** Greek Prepositions

| Preposition | Genitive (Ablatival) | Dative (Instrumental) | Accusative |
|---|---|---|---|
| ἀμφί | concerning | — | about, around |
| ἀνά | — | — | up along, up |
| ἀντί | instead of, for | — | — |
| ἀπό | from | — | — |
| διά | through | — | through, because of |
| εἰς ~ ἐς | — | — | into |
| ἐκ ~ ἐξ | out of | — | |
| ἐν | — | in, among (loc.) | — |
| ἐπί | on, atop | on, near, at, by | on, against |
| κατά | down from [cf. ἀνά] | — | down, by *distributive* |
| μετά | with | — | after |
| παρά | beside, from the side of | at, at the side of | to the side of, compared with |
| περί | about, concerning | — | about, near |
| πρό | before | — | — |
| πρός | toward, to | at, near, in addition to | to, with reference to, against |
| σύν ~ ξύν | — | with, by aid of | — |
| ὑπέρ | above, on behalf of | — | over, exceeding |
| ὑπό | under, through *cause, agent* | under *static* | under *motion* |

## Possession: Belonging and owning

To this point, we have not discussed the genitive much, other than as the Greek expression of its ancestral ablative. The two main functions of the genitive, however—the *possessive* and the *partitive*—can be viewed as the logical forebears of all the remaining truly genitival constructions (as opposed to the ablatival genitives, which are also extremely important in Greek; they don't occur in Latin).

The genitive seems most comfortable as a kind of substitute for the attributive adjective. Genitives are much less likely, in either Greek or Latin, to anchor the main predicate of a clause or a sentence. In such situations, both languages are much more likely to use the dative, which expresses the idea relationally:

> Mihi nomen est C. Iulius Caesar.
>
> *To me [the] name is C. Julius Caesar.*
>
> *(I.e., My name is C. Julius Caesar.)*

Greek uses the parallel construction:

ὄνομα μοί ἐστι . . .

ἔδοξα ἀκοῦσαι ὄνομα αὐτῷ εἶναι Ἀγάθωνα

*I thought I heard his name was Agathon.*

—Plato, *Protagoras* 315e

In both Greek and Latin, the dative construction is more idiomatic than one with the possessive adjective/pronoun (*nomen meum*); the use of the genitive of the personal pronoun (*nomen mei*), while logically unassailable, is virtually unheard of (no more idiomatic in Latin than "the name of me" would be in English).

Still, with a different verb, a genitive is entirely possible:

Δαρείου καὶ Παρυσάτιδος γίγνονται παῖδες δύο.

*Of (or from) Darius and Parysatis are [born] two sons.*

*(I.e., Darius and Parysatis have two sons.)*

*(Or simply) There are two sons of Darius and Parysatis.*

—Xenophon, *Anabasis* 1.1.1

Within the larger field of possession, there are many cases that are felt, by virtue of the verb, to be predisposed toward one or the other construction. A word like ἄρχω, "I rule," so strongly favors the genitive that it would be quite odd to say:

Cyrus was the ruler to that region.

—that is, using a dative. There are many other similar situations in Latin. Ultimately, there is no absolute rule to govern all these lexical peculiarities.

Where the word modified by the genitive noun is itself an abstract noun representing some kind of *verbal* idea—that is, an action (particularly a transitive one), another set of important categories raises its head. We can talk about these modifying genitives as either *objective* or *subjective*. This is occasionally intimidating to students, but the underlying concept is simple enough. They are distinguished one from another by context alone; functionally, one (the subjective genitive) represents the *subject* of an action implicit in the word modified, and the other the *object*.

In English we tend to separate these loosely by using the possessive for the subjective genitive and a prepositional phrase with "of" for the objective genitive, though this is by no means a hard rule. In any case, in Greek and Latin, a phrase like φιλία τοῦ πατρός

amor patris

*[the] love of a father*

can refer *either* to the father's love for his children *or* to a child's love for a father. Neither is absolutely more correct than the other; context is the only rational determinant here.

## The partitive

Akin to the possessive genitive is the *partitive* genitive. It's not entirely different in its impulse, but it is distinct enough to be classified as something separate, and it's useful to learn to recognize it. The partitive genitive expresses the *whole* of which we are talking about a *part*. Thus:

The lid of a box

. . . ὃς νῦν πολλὸν ἄριστος Ἀχαιῶν εὔχεται εἶναι

*. . . who now boasts that he is by far the best of the Achaeans*

—Homer, *Iliad* 1.91

## Material, measure, and quality

*Genitives of material, quality, contents, measure, price, value*, and the like are without conflicting uses in the other cases, and mostly they correspond very closely to English forms. They are still not entirely without complications, however, and are used with some subtlety. In the simplest forms they seem intuitively obvious to English speakers:

Romulus made an altar of stone. (genitival)
Romulus made an altar from [out of] stone. (ablatival, separative)

Both Greek and Latin use the same construction, which is not overly surprising. In Latin, in particular, the genitive of quality comes with its own peculiar wrinkle: the genitive of permanent quality is frequent enough, but it will virtually never appear without a modifying adjective. Thus one can say:

Fuit vir magnae fortitudinis.

*He was a man of great strength.*

but not

> Fuit vir fortitudinis.
>
> *He was a man of strength.*

The latter usage seems a bit strange even in English, but few speakers can really identify why, or what it would need to make it sound normal to their ears. My own conjecture is that the unaccompanied genitive of quality would, to a native Latin-speaker, sound like noninformation. We would perceive it the same way in some cases, but not others. To us, "He was a man of strength" sounds reasonable, but we would probably not say: "He was a man of height." Everyone is a person of *some* height or other; telling us that would be pointless. The quantifier *is* the actual information here; without it we're simply building a frame of reference and then not filling it.

When used to describe material or contents, the genitive is usually used more or less the same way an attributive adjective is used, but it can be a predicate as well. It may be literal or figurative:

> The table was of wood. (material, literal)
> She had a will of iron. (material, metaphorical)
> I gave her a glass of water. (contents)

Akin to this use, but formally distinct from it, is the genitive of price or value:

> We usually buy gasoline at a high price. (I.e., "of a high price")
> It costs three talents a gallon. (I.e., "of three talents")

Similar to this too is the genitive of measure, which is not very different from the genitive of quality discussed above:

> It was a staff of seven feet.

In the case of certain verbs of perceiving, Greek is particularly exact in using the partitive genitive of the thing perceived—especially in the case of hearing. Hence, while we normally have

> I saw the wolf.

for hearing, we find both of the following:

> I heard the trumpet. (I.e. "of the trumpet," genitive)
> I heard the trumpet. (accusative)

which mean more or less the same thing in such a context. The partitive construction would not normally be used for hearing *about* something, however; for that in Greek one would use a prepositional phrase with περί. The fundamental idea driving the use of the genitive with ἀκούω or the like seems to be in differentiating the trumpet *itself* from its sound, which is *of* or *from* the trumpet. One cannot hear the trumpet directly: one hears only its output. The distinction may seem overly fastidious in English, since there seems to be no other way to hear a trumpet than to hear the sound that it makes, but the idea is not at least in itself irrational.

Arguably this use of the genitive is more fundamentally ablatival than genitival—it has to do with the sound being something that comes *from* or *out of* the trumpet. It's included here among the genitive constructions for convenience.

## Relation

As noted above, the dative case is primarily about relationship and relevance; almost every one of the catalog of dative constructions—*indirect object, advantage and disadvantage, the ethical dative*, and so on—can be boiled down to this single central idea. By historical time some of these functions have been taken over by prepositional constructions, but the dative remains robust and useful. It's the subjectivizing element, one might argue: most instances of the dative will express, one way or another, the *person to whom* (much less frequently the *thing to which*) the predication is relevant or true. Grasping this central concept really will rationalize most of the constructions that grammars catalog separately.

The so-called *dative of agent* in Greek or Latin is a case in point. To think of it as being anything like the *genitive* or *ablative of agent* with passive verbs is to misunderstand how it means what it means. Allen and Greenough (§374, n. 2) argue that the Latin version is "either a special case of the Dative of Possession or a development of the Dative of Reference." There seems to me to be little doubt that it's the latter.

The Greek dative of agent is generally confined to the perfect forms of the verb, which (as has been discussed above) reflect the *resulting state or condition* derived from the verbal activity. It also shows up with verbal adjectives in -τος and -τεος, reflecting the obligation to do something. In both cases, therefore, it is similarly relational—specifying *to or for whom* something is in a having-been-completed condition, or *to or for whom* it remains to be accomplished:

οἱ δὲ Κορίνθιοι, ἐπειδὴ **αὐτοῖς** παρεσκεύαστο, ἔπλεον ἐπὶ τὴν Κέρκυραν ναυσὶ πεντήκοντα καὶ ἑκατόν.

*But the Corinthians, when the preparations were in a having-been-completed condition respecting them, sailed to Corcyra with 150 ships.*

*(I.e., ... when preparations had been made by them ... )*

—Thucydides, Peloponnesian War 1.46

... ἡμῖν γ᾽ ὑπὲρ τῆς ἐλευθερίας ἀγωνιστέον.

*... for us, at least, it is necessary to fight for the sake of liberty.*

*(I.e., ... but we, at least, must fight for liberty.)*

—Demosthenes, *Philippic* 3.70

The Latin dative of agent is similar, though it tends to be confined to the gerund and gerundive forms—akin, therefore, to the Greek verbal adjectives in -τος and -τεος:

... itaque haec **vobis** provincia, Quirites ... non modo a calamitate sed etiam a metu calamitatis est defendenda.

*... therefore this province is in a to-be-defended condition for you, Romans ... not only from disaster but from the fear of disaster.*

*(I.e., ... therefore you must defend this province, Romans ... )*

—Cicero, *On Pompey's Command* 14

### Respect

Seemingly akin to the relational constructions recounted above are *constructions of respect*. These are concerned with restricting the scope of a predication, not in terms of the *person* to whom it's relevant, but the area or sphere of understanding that defines it.

The fact that these constructions most typically fall to the dative in Greek and to the ablative in Latin, it may be reasonable to assume that at least this form of the construction is an outgrowth of the instrumental—that is, that its original formulation expresses the means by which something is true.

Somewhat more difficult to account for is the accusative of respect in Greek (which is also adopted into Latin on occasion—probably as a deliberate Hellenizing feature). It may be an outgrowth of a more generic adverbial accusative, but it would be hard to establish that rigorously.

Overall their uses do not seem to differ greatly. The dative of respect (the first example below) is rather similar to the accusative of respect (the second example):

καὶ γὰρ ὁρᾶν στυγνὸς ἦν καὶ τῇ **φωνῇ** τραχύς . . .

*for he was gloomy to look at and harsh in [respect to his] voice . . .*

—Xenophon, *Anabasis* 2.6.9

τοῖσι δ᾽ ἀνιστάμενος μετέφη **πόδας** ὠκὺς Ἀχιλλεύς . . .

*Standing forth before them, Achilles swift with respect to his feet said . . .*

*(I.e., . . . swift-footed Achilles said . . . )*

—Homer, *Iliad* 1.58

You can see how closely the Latin *ablative of respect* (sometimes called the *ablative of specification*) echoes these constructions, and is used for virtually the same kinds of referents:

. . . **lingua** haesitantes, **voce** absoni . . .

*. . . halting in [respect to their] speech, and harsh in [respect to their] voice . . .*

—Cicero, *On the Orator* 1.115

Nam et **statura** fuit humili et **corpore** exiguo et claudus **altero pede**.

*For he was short in [respect to his] stature and slight in [respect to his] body and lame in [respect to] one foot.*

—Nepos, *Agesilaus* 8

### Cause

An example of a causal construction is as follows:

Crossing the river was hard on account of the flood.

Most frequently in both Greek and Latin, this concept will be expressed with a prepositional phrase. The bare ablative of cause in Latin is nevertheless attested. To many students this may seem to correspond to the instrumental sense of the case. In fact, however, the corresponding Greek version is in the genitive, which suggests instead an ablatival or separative notion of causation—specifically, denoting the situation *out of which* something else emerges. In this regard, these constructions may conservatively prefigure the more freewheeling absolutes, discussed at the end of this chapter:

εὐδαίμων γάρ μοι ἀνὴρ ἐφαίνετο, ὦ Ἐχέκρατες, καὶ **τοῦ τρόπου** καὶ **τῶν λόγων.**

*The man seemed to be happy to me, both from [on account of] his character and from [on account of] his words.*

—Plato, *Phaedo* 58e

multis in rebus **neglegentia** plectimur . . .

*we are punished from [on account of] our negligence in many spheres . . .*

—Cicero, *On Friendship* 85

### Adverbial accusative

It is hard to construct a compelling rationale to account for the *adverbial accusative*, other than to trace it back to the idea that it provides a limiting condition (hence, metaphorically, a goal of motion) for the predication in question. It can be used with nouns, pronouns, and adjectives. Compare the English usage with adjectives and nouns to form the adverbial sense:

They went the quickest way.

*(I.e., . . . by [means of] the quickest way)*

Greek uses the accusative for this kind of construction:

τὴν ταχίστην (ὁδόν)

English adjectives and nouns, being unmarked for case, don't make the distinction. The neuter interrogative pronoun (esp. with an intransitive verb) for *why* can also be understood as an adverbial accusative:

**τί** ἦλθεν;

*Why [i.e., (for) what] did he come?*

ὁ Μεγαβάτης . . . ἔπλεε **πρόφασιν** ἐπ᾽ Ἑλλησπόντου . . .

*Then Megabates . . . sailed [as] **a pretext** to the Hellespont . . .*

—Herodotus, *Histories* 5. 33; trans. A. D. Godley

## Cognate accusative

The *cognate accusative* draws the action of the verb out to form a pseudo-object, often used with a verb that is actually intransitive in sense, sometimes not. It is somewhat similar to the *accusative of respect* or *adverbial accusative*:

> He fought the good fight. (not in the same sense as "against the good fight," which is the usual sense of an accusative object of "fight")
>
> He walked his aimless walk. (object of an otherwise intransitive verb)

## Agency with passive verbs

It is fairly common for students learning elementary Latin to confuse the *constructions of personal agent* with the *instrumental*. There is of course a certain apparent similarity in concept, since the *means by which* something is done is arguably akin to the *agent by whom* it is done. Students often think of the Latin *ablative of personal agent* as a kind of specialized case of the *instrumental ablative*, therefore, though it comes oddly fitted out with the preposition *ab*. Some grammars reinforce this perception.

If the historical principles I've been suggesting here are valid, however, it's a mistaken perception. Comparison of the Latin and Greek constructions will bring the matter into focus. In Greek, personal agency is accomplished with the preposition ὑπό followed (as ὑπό invariably is) by the *genitive*. If both of these have derived from the same source—something of a leap of faith, but seemingly supported by the evidence—the comparison highlights an intriguing difference. The fact that the *instrumental* construction is achieved with the ablative in Latin and with the dative in Greek confirms the fairly obvious notion that the parent construction was instrumental too: what else would we expect? The fact that the Greek *personal-agent* construction employs the genitive, however, suggests instead an ancestral true *ablative* construction—that is, a separative one, bespeaking not instrumentality but *source*. Further bolstering this notion is the fact that in poetic usage the *genitive of agent* will occasionally appear without any preposition:

> . . . σὺ δ' ἐν Ἀΐδα
> κεῖσαι, σᾶς ἀλόχου σφαγαῖς
> Αἰγίσθου τ', Ἀγάμεμνον.

> . . . *But you, Agamemnon, lie in Hades, by the butchery of your wife and Aegisthus.*
>
> —Euripides, *Electra* 122–24

I would go further, and suggest that this is in fact of a piece with what has been said earlier about the *accusative direct object* as an outgrowth of the goal-of-motion construction. If in fact the notion of transitivity is ultimately a figurative extension of the physical and spatial notion of movement *toward* or *at* someone or something, the agent construction forms a complement to that idea, rooted in a similar abstraction of motion *from*. It's about where the action *comes from*. On this view, I would argue, the agent construction takes on a more rational, though earthier, vigor—and distinguishing it from the instrumental construction is simple.

**The absolute: A tentative interpretation**

Both Greek and Latin have *absolute* constructions that are often seen as perversely difficult. The basic rule of the absolute is that it is precisely that—absolute: that is, it must be unattached. By this, grammarians mean that it must not be tied to any other word or phrase in the sentence in which it occurs. (There are occasional exceptions, even in good authors, but they are rare, and usually betoken a loss of focus, or a confusion about where the sentence is going.) The *ablative absolute* in Latin and the *genitive absolute* in Greek normally express something about the *surrounding circumstances*, however. Sometimes this construction is even referred to as the *ablative (or genitive) of attendant circumstance*.

The suggestive power of the absolute construction would be hard to overestimate. It is capable of "hanging" or "floating" a secondary thought over a sentence in a kind of semantic cloud, while refusing to specify just how the one idea is to be connected to the other. It is capable, moreover, of planting an idea without taking responsibility for the reader's apprehension of it.

> Caesare duce, Vercingetorix victus est.

literally means only

> *Caesar [being] general, Vercingetorix was conquered.*

It is up to the reader to decide whether this means

> **Because** Caesar was the general, Vercingetorix was conquered.

or

> **When** Caesar was the general, Vercingetorix was conquered.

or even (theoretically)

> **Although** Caesar was the general, Vercingetorix was conquered.

Any of those is a legitimate interpretation of the absolute; none of them is compelling. The ambiguity is intrinsic to the construction itself. Certain authors employ it rather freely; others use it with clinical precision to plant doubt and nurture ambiguity. Some well-meaning teachers insist that absolutes always be translated analytically—that is, providing some resolution to the ambiguity. But if an author has used it precisely to create and foster ambiguity, an unambiguous translation overlooks at least one potential *point* of the absolute, and hence obscures the author's intention by flattening it to a single choice.

Some grammarians have been at pains to identify what the Greek and Latin absolute constructions are about and where they come from, but I'm not entirely comfortable with their conclusions. Allen and Greenough's generally reliable grammar of Latin argues that the ablative absolute is "perhaps of *instrumental* origin. It is, however, sometimes explained as an outgrowth of the *locative*, and in any event certain locative constructions (of *place* and *time*) must have contributed to its development." E. C. Woodcock (*A New Latin Syntax*) considers the ablative absolute to be a special case of the ablative of attendant circumstance, which seems defensible, but clusters it among the "sociative-instrumental" functions of the ablative (§§43, 49).

I disagree. It seems to me that the fact that the answering construction in Greek is *not* a dative but a *genitive* absolute clearly indicates that this usage is of *ablatival* origin. To revert once again to drawing these figures of thought from a physical analogue, I think one can best apprehend its meaning in terms of separation or emergence. In other words, the ablative or genitive absolute represents a circumstance that is to be understood as more *generative* than attendant—the *source or context from which* the specific action of the sentence's main predication arises. Viewed in this way, the absolute becomes a good deal more consistent, and even its ambiguity—which allows it to range from causal to concessive and back again—can be brought under control.

> Caesare duce, Vercingetorix victus est.

becomes something more like

> **From** Caesar [being] general, [it emerged that] Vercingetorix was conquered.

Understanding the absolute construction as being fundamentally about source and context, rather than something else, will also account for the fact that it is absolute without that being an artificial or arbitrary stricture. Few rules in natural language really arise for no reason; fewer still will endure under those circumstances. Instead, I would argue that the "absoluteness" naturally expresses the fact that nothing can reasonably be understood as *coming forth from itself*. As long as one grasps it on these terms, the canonical separation from the other elements of the sentence is virtually inevitable. In later Latin and Greek, the critical erosion of the absolute probably documents as clearly as anything could the final breakdown of that intuitively separative understanding.

# CHAPTER 9

# Verbal Nouns and Adjectives

*Words that come from verbs and can slide into other roles*

## Nouns

On the ancient definition of the term, the so-called verbals are verbal nouns. That is, they are verbs that have been rendered into some noun form—but "noun" in this sense refers to both substantives and adjectives.

In practical terms, however, we may distinguish verbal adjectives from verbal substantives—what are usually referred to in English usage as verbal nouns. There are two kinds of verbal substantives (the infinitive and the gerund) in general use in English and Latin, though there is only one in Greek; the verbal adjective is always the participle, though the range of possible participles varies hugely. English and Latin have fairly limited participles; Greek has a vast and robust system of participles that do a good deal of the heavy lifting of the language.

We've already sketched an outline of how these work. Since verbals arguably function as either substantives or adjectives, one can confidently assert that this is, fundamentally, what they *are*, but, at the same time, they have certain super-powers not granted to normal mortal nouns and adjectives. No other nouns, for example, are marked for tense or for voice. (Verbals are not normally marked for mood, and indeed, the form of the verbal—infinitive, gerund, or participle—is often classed as a kind of pseudomood of its own; they are not marked for person, either.) Participles *are* marked for number, but in this respect they are not particularly different from other adjectives. Substantive verbals—infinitives and gerunds—are all considered singular in Latin and Greek. (Neither language seems to have considered a plural gerund, like the occasionally heard English "comings and goings.")

Verbals can often also take objects, and certainly the range of possibilities attaching to the Greek participle, vast as it is, is enormous.

# Infinitives

The simplest verbal substantive is the infinitive. People often don't even think of it as being a noun, but as a strange form of the verb that they just use in certain situations. It typically is used to complement other verbs, is sometimes used with verbs of speaking to express indirect speech, and at other times approaches the normal use of the noun.

In fact it is always a noun. In English we have a synthetic infinitive, invariably made of "to" followed by the verb itself:

> to run
> to say
> to hit

The reasons for this curious formulation are matters of historical Germanic linguistics. Old English had a simple one-word infinitive, as does modern German. The fact that the English infinitive is a composite of two words is the source of the anxiety surrounding the so-called split infinitive: according to some stylists (especially of the nineteenth and early twentieth centuries) it was unacceptable to separate the "to" from the verb itself with any intervening words. There are a number of reasons for this, some of them good. Some have claimed that the insistence derives from Latin usage, since Latin infinitives, being only one word, cannot possibly be split. This seems a somewhat dubious explanation on examination, since Latin's very inability to split its infinitive would have precluded any special rules arising in this regard.

The prohibition against the split infinitive is one of those apparently arbitrary rules that has been ignored by good authors since the earliest days of modern English. Shakespeare gleefully (and probably unconsciously) splits infinitives in plays and poems. Modern authors do the same. *Star Trek* enshrined in the language the catchphrase "to boldly go where no man has gone before." (Subsequent versions of that show, catering to more modern sensibilities, changed the language that was considered sexist, but the split infinitive remains: "to boldly go where no one has gone before.") Concern for the split infinitive is probably now at an all-time low.

That being said, it's arguable that *in general*, without making it a cause of undue anxiety, avoiding split infinitives is probably a good idea. There are two reasons.

First, the farther the "to" is removed from its verb, the longer the hearer or reader has to bear in mind the fact that an infinitive is on the way—or, more accurately, in the works. In the era of attention spans fine-tuned by television and the Internet, that may be overly taxing.

Second, and perhaps more serious, is the fact that "to" has a perfectly respectable life as a preposition, and the farther it gets from its verb, the more likely it is to be misconstrued that way. In spoken language the problem is trebled: "to" is not normally *pronounced* very differently from "too" or "two," and any or all of those meanings could spontaneously emerge from an unattached prepositional or infinitival "to." Accordingly I normally encourage my students *not* to split infinitives—not out of my (admitted) native stodginess, but in the simple interest of clarity.

None of this is a problem in Greek or Latin, since they have one-word infinitives:

| | | |
|---|---|---|
| laudare | habuisse | παιδεύειν |
| παῦσαι | διαλέγεσθαι | |

As noted, the infinitive retains certain of the functional properties of the verb, inasmuch as it can still be marked for tense or take objects:

to have run
to be going to run
to have said this
to hit the baseball

These are not among the normal capacities of nouns, considered simply. This is one of the reasons that verbals can occasionally be tricky and difficult to analyze.

Greek has promoted the infinitive to a more flexible tool than either Latin or English by the so-called *articular* infinitive. The articular infinitive is simply an infinitive (which is regarded as a neuter singular noun) bound up with an article. Thus the infinitive παιδεύειν can be rendered in any of the four cases of Greek:

τὸ παιδεύειν
τοῦ παιδεύειν
τῷ παιδεύειν
τὸ παιδεύειν

The infinitive itself undergoes no change, but the case is indicated by the article. Of course the first and last forms here are identical, but the context seldom leaves much ambiguity about how the infinitive is to be taken. Accordingly τὸ παιδεύειν would be used as we use either the infinitive or the gerund in English as subject:

ἀγαθὸν τὸ παιδεύειν

*To teach [is] good.*

or

*Teaching [is] good.*

It may also appear as an object or in any other function in a sentence:

τοῦ παιδεύειν

*of teaching*

τῷ παιδεύειν

*for teaching, by means of teaching*

τὸ παιδεύειν

*teaching (as object)*

The articular infinitive accordingly obviates any need for a gerund in Greek, and, as was mentioned earlier, there is none.

# Gerunds

The gerund is perhaps the least-understood English verb form, and people are confused about it in Latin as well. Adding to the confusion is the fact that in English it looks exactly like the present active participle. In the sentence

Swimming is prohibited.

the word "swimming" is a gerund.

In the sentence

I saw the man swimming.

"swimming" is a participle. This of course perplexes people, but the difference is one of function: the gerund is a *noun* (substantive). It is capable of standing as a subject, as in the first example, or as an object:

I like swimming.

The participle, which we will discuss shortly, is an *adjective*, though a uniquely powerful one with a number of extra abilities.

The English gerund is used more or less interchangeably with the infinitive; though it is a little more stilted, it would not be ungrammatical to say:

> To swim is prohibited.

It would not even seem stilted to say:

> I like to swim.

The infinitive can do some things that the gerund cannot, and the gerund can do a few things that the infinitive cannot, but in general they divide the field somewhat chaotically and redundantly in English. Many of the places where complementary infinitives can be used, the gerund can slide into place:

> He began swimming.

Not so in Latin. The infinitive and the gerund divide the duties of verbal noun neatly between them. The infinitive is treated as a neuter verbal noun, but because the infinitive is not inflected any further, there would be no way to tell—either positionally or otherwise—whether it was serving as a subject (nominative) or as an object or possessive in another case. Accordingly, the infinitive is reserved for the nominative, while the gerund takes up the other cases. As elsewhere, the Latin gerund is not inflected for number; it is always a singular neuter noun. These gerunds can do things that are normally characteristic of verbs, such as taking objects.

That being said, it should be noted that Classical Latin generally chafes at abstract nouns, and there is a decided tendency to *avoid* the gerund when it is possible and reasonable to do so. The same cannot be said for Medieval Latin, which developed an almost diametrically opposite delight in abstract nouns (including gerunds). These become the staple of Scholastic thought, and authors such as Thomas Aquinas, Duns Scotus, and William of Ockham use them routinely.

Greek is able to do without the gerund altogether, since the articular infinitive is so flexible. Any infinitive can be put into any case required, merely by bundling it up with the relevant article.

## The mighty participle

The participle is, from the ancient point of view, also a verbal noun—but a verbal *adjective* as opposed to a verbal *substantive*. However you classify them, participles are, like gerunds and infinitives, capable of taking on some of the distinctive markings of verbs, and also of pointing to objects and of being modified by adverbs and adverbial clauses or phrases.

The English participles form a rather spare set. We have a present active participle and a perfect passive participle, and that's about it. The present active form looks just like the gerund, but it's used differently. In weak verbs the perfect participle tends to be the same form as the active participle, but with "-ed" rather than "-ing" on the end. In strong verbs often the root itself undergoes change, often with "-en" for the perfect passive participle. Hence:

> Facilitate, facilitating, facilitated
> Break, breaking, broken

It's important to differentiate the present active participle from the gerund in practice. There's no way to do so by merely looking at the word in isolation, but by taking the context carefully into consideration, it's usually not particularly hard. There are a few tough boundary cases, and we'll take those up shortly.

In English, then, we have two kinds of participles—active and passive. Strictly speaking, English participles are marked for tense, too: the active participle is present, and the passive participle is past (arguably perfect). In this regard the names of the forms and their broadest functions are more or less the same as those of Latin. But in practice the distinctions of tense and voice are weaker; we can turn our perfect passive participle ("broken") into a present passive participle by the addition of "being":

> The wall was broken [i.e., it was in a broken state; it had been broken already].
> The wall was being broken [i.e., the process was going on].

This pattern is not as easily applicable to all situations, however. While one can use the perfect passive participle attributively:

> The broken wall was covered with ivy.

it's not as easy to import the "being" variation into the attributive situation:

> The being broken wall was covered with ivy.

One might plausibly say:

> The wall, being broken, was covered with ivy.

but the commas tell us that "being broken" is a parenthetical modifier. If we left the commas out, it would effectively turn into a compressed relative clause:

> The wall [that was] being broken was covered with ivy.

In an oddly nonparallel construction, moreover, we can create a composite perfect active participle, but to do so we couple the auxiliary verb "having" with the *passive* rather than the active participle. This shows the active form:

> The Goths storming the city met fierce resistance.

The compound past active form can be seen in this example:

> Having stormed the city, the Goths went away with their plunder.

All of which, perhaps, argues merely that our relationship with our English participles is very complex, and laden with potential ambiguities and pitfalls.

More problematic for our purposes here, a foggy apprehension of how the English participle works will tend to slop over into our understanding of the participle in Latin and Greek, and that's usually not helpful. Probably a majority of students learning elementary Latin have some difficulty embracing the notion that the perfect passive participle in Latin *really is* perfect, and not equally at home as a present. But it's not.

## Not quite participles

We mentioned the problem of words that *look* like participles—really derived from a verb, really ending in "-ing," *and* really acting as adjectives, but still not really functioning as participles. This issue gets past even some grammarians, and I have seen examples in books that purport to be teaching grammar (in one way or another) that have failed to distinguish them altogether.

The word "running" is a participle when used in sentences like these:

> The police apprehended the running man.
> I saw the man running down the street.

The first of these is what we call an attibutive use of the participle, while the second one is circumstantial, but they're both participles. On the other hand, "running" is *not* really a participle when used in a sentence like the following:

> I bought a new pair of running shoes yesterday.

Why? For the simple reason that the shoes *were not in fact running* when you bought them. One indicator is the fact that one could not reverse the order without destroying the meaning:

> I saw a pair of shoes running.

This "running" would be a participle, but it clearly doesn't mean the same thing as the previous version.

In an expression like "running shoes," the word "running" is not really a participle, but a gerund, operating very much the same way other nouns operate quasi-adjectivally, as domain-restricting modifiers (e.g., "baseball bat," "track shoes," "peanut butter").

These gerunds are often mistaken for participles by those who are too zealously following the principle that says that if an "-ing" word is modifying a noun, it must be a participle, and if not, it must be a gerund. Such rules may be convenient, but they are no substitute for an understanding of the actual functions of the two kinds of words—an understanding that most of us have instinctively, even if we don't consciously think of it in grammatical terms. This can be verified in casual conversation with almost any native English-speaker. In normal English speech, unless there is some other special reason to modify the stress, such a noun functioning as a domain-modifier (not really an adjective, but close) is almost invariably accented more heavily than the noun it precedes. We would say:

> I would like some fresh **butter**.

but

> I would like some **peanut** butter.

or

> He was swinging an old **bat**.

but

> He was able to defend himself only with an old **baseball** bat.

The same principle distinguishes the true participle from such a restrictive gerund in attributive position. The difference in pronunciation reflects our functional understanding. We *would say*:

> I bought a new pair of **running** shoes.

but

> I don't seem to be able to find a running **car**.

or

> I have cleaned up the old **frying** pan.

but

> This painting looks like a frying **egg**.

In written text, there is no emphasis to mark the distinction, so we must rely on context and our sense of the passage.

One curious example arises in the Latin translation by Peter Needham of J. K. Rowling's *Harry Potter and the Philosopher's Stone*. There we are introduced, as readers of the book or viewers of the movie may recall, to the Sorting Hat. I had always taken the word "sorting" here as a restrictive gerund modifer like those above—akin to "running" in "running shoes." I would refer to it as

the **Sorting** Hat.

Needham clearly took this the other way, and translated it with the Latin present participle—not normally used for this kind of thing—as

Petasus Distribuens.

To my eye, this suggests a hat that is (perhaps perpetually, or at least at the moment when we're discussing it) engaged in sorting. Certainly, according to the story, it does indeed sort the students into their various houses. I had assumed, however, that, like running shoes (which never actually run on their own, but are running shoes even in the box), it remained the Sorting Hat even while singing a song or sitting on a shelf. To my eye, the more characteristic Latin rendition (perhaps colored by my background in Medieval Latin) would have been

Petasus Distribuendi

—that is, effectively,

*[the] Hat **of Sorting***.

Such subtleties afford considerable room for speculation and amusement, though there may be no single right answer to them.

### Dangling participles and why they're (sometimes) funny

Probably the most famous participial phenomenon in English is the so-called dangling participle. It's not really a construction so much as an error, but hovers in the murky air between syntax and semantics, and can often successfully convey something you don't want it to convey. It can crop up, moreover, even in the work of experienced writers and native speakers.

Because English participles are not marked for case, number, or gender (as Latin and Greek participles are), the only way to determine what they are modifying is to rely on position. In general, the rule of thumb (sometimes but not always superseded by common sense) is that it should be construed with the nearest noun. When proximity is in doubt, or when the rule is simply ignored, careless participle placement can result in such comical visions as

> I saw the new stadium driving into town last week.

Assuming a rational but grammatically shaky speaker, rather than a precise but delusional one, we probably can figure out that the meaning here would be more clearly expressed as

> Driving into the city last week, I saw the new stadium.

Alternatively, one could break it out into a clause, which would solve the problem just as conclusively, but by a different method:

> I saw the new stadium while I was driving into town last week.

Surely nobody in his or her right mind has ever seen a stadium driving into the city or anywhere else.

If you keep your eye open for them, you can collect a list of very amusing dangling participles pretty quickly. The problem becomes a more serious impediment to communication when it's not comical, because common sense doesn't correct it for you. But the ambiguity may lead to genuine misunderstanding:

> I saw Jane driving into the city last week.

This is perfectly reasonable, but it is not at all the same thing as when the participle modifies the pronoun:

> Driving into the city last week, I saw Jane.

If one uses one where one intends the other—either way—misunderstanding almost certainly will ensue. It may or may not be hilarious, depending on the gravity of the subject matter. Clearly,

> Kissing my wife, I surprised your husband.

might be only a bit of social chitchat, while a misplaced participle turns it into the stuff of tragedy or at least soap opera:

> I surprised your husband kissing my wife.

## Latin: The limited participle

Latin has a more developed system of participles than does English, though its inventory of options is still rather small compared with those of Greek. Still, Latin grew to literary maturity in the shadow of Greek, and Latin authors were constantly striving to emulate Greek models; this led them to push the boundaries of the available participial constructions fairly hard, with varying success.

Latin has a present active and a perfect passive participle. They are used extensively in all periods. It also has future active and passive participles, which are somewhat less common, but still in play over most of the history of the language. That admits four tense/voice combinations in all. There are some who would dispute the designation of the gerundive as a participle, but it is handled as one (future passive). There seems no reason not to classify it as such. Hence we have forms like the following:

> laudaturus
>
> *about to / going to praise*
>
> laudandus
>
> *about to be / going to be praised*

Future participles have some special implications. The future active participle often provides a compact alternative to the adverbial purpose clause:

> Venio Caesarem laudaturus.
>
> *I come [being] about to praise Caesar.*
>
> *(I.e., I come [in order] to praise Caesar.)*

The future passive participle, on the other hand, is most often (though not exclusively) used to express necessity or obligation:

> Caesar laudandus est.
>
> *Caesar is about to be praised.*
>
> *(I.e., Caesar is in an about-to-be praised state.)*

Implicitly, this often means

> Caesar ought to be praised.
> Caesar should be praised.

All these forms are so common that they need to be mastered as normal ways of saying these things. The presence of participles in composite verb forms is also interesting, but most elementary Latin textbooks cover that issue thoroughly enough that it needs no further discussion here.

## Greek: The unlimited participle

With Greek we find a system of participles that extends into virtually every corner of the language experience and allows us to express a vast range of actions, experiences, motivations, and entailed propositions without resorting to a complete clause. The Greek participial system is enormous, and while its syntax is not especially problematic, it does have some considerable nuance. Greek has participles in the present, aorist, perfect, and future tenses (though not the imperfect, pluperfect, or future perfect). Many of these exist in active, middle, and passive forms, though some appear in only one or two voices.

Participles can be used to convey all manner of things, and in idiomatic Attic Greek they often carry a burden that English-speaking students find daunting. Often one needs to resort to a whole clause in order to express their meanings accurately in English. More interesting still is the fact that the Greek participle will often carry what seems to us to be the main semantic burden of a sentence (that is, what we would translate as the main verb), while the main verb of the sentence (there still must be one) is relegated to second-class status. Aeschylus provides a typical example; Orestes is standing at the tomb of his father Agamemnon:

> οὐ γὰρ παρὼν ᾤμωξα σόν, πάτερ, μόρον
> οὐδ᾽ ἐξέτεινα χεῖρ᾽ ἐπ᾽ ἐκφορᾷ νεκροῦ.

> —Aeschylus, *The Libation Bearers* 8–9

Literally, that would be the following:

> *I did not lament your death, father, being present,*
> *Nor extend my hand for the bearing of [your] body.*

In more normal idiomatic English terms, though, respecting the lifting power of the Greek participle, that would probably be better rendered:

> *I was not present, father, to lament your death,*
> *Or extend my hand to bear your body.*

The emphasis has distinctly changed. Certainly the fundamental problem for Orestes is not that he had been present, but had failed to perform the rites, but that he was *not* present, and on that account he was not able to perform them.

The morphology of the Greek participles is prodigious, but beyond the scope of this book, which concerns itself with syntax. The *uses* of Greek participles, however, can be broken down into three broad classes—the *attributive*, the *circumstantial*, and the *supplementary*.

### Attributive participles

An attributive participle functions as an adjective in the normal way. Greek flags attributive adjectives of all sorts by tucking them in between the article and the noun to be modified, and that it does so with these participles simply validates the approach to them. Hence we find such things as this:

> . . . καὶ τὸν **ἐφεστηκότα** κίνδυνον τῇ πόλει διαλύσειν.
>
> . . . *and that I am dispelling the danger* **threatening** *the city.*
>
>                    —Demosthenes, *On the Crown* 176

More interesting yet is the fact that the word to be modified may be omitted, if it has an article and clearly refers to a person or a thing (that is, the adjective—in this case a participle—is being substantivized):

> ὁ ταῦτα λέγων
>
> *the saying-these-things [one]*
>
> (*I.e., the one saying these things; the one who is saying these things*)

In doing so, it is fully capable of replacing relative clauses with a construction of equal power and precision, though without using a clause.

### Circumstantial participles

The circumstantial participle conveys something about the circumstances surrounding the action of the main verb of the clause in which the participial phrase is found. It is not attributed narrowly to a noun to be modified, though it does in some sense modify the noun. It is distinguished by not being put after an article, and it effectively forms an adverbial phrase:

> ταῦτα λέγων ἀπέθανεν.
>
> *[While] saying these things, he died.*
>
> ταῦτα εἴπων ἀπέθανεν.
>
> *Having said these things, he died.*
>
> ταῦτα λέξων ἀπέθανεν.
>
> *Being about to say [or intending to say] these things, he died.*

The only thing that has changed here is the tense of the participle itself. Greek writers were normally rather fastidious about their tenses. In English we might say:

> Saying these things, he died.

meaning that he said these things and then died. Good Greek and Latin authors normally will not: they will almost always use the aorist (Greek) or the perfect (Latin) participle to convey the idea of action before that of the main verb. A present participle is understood to refer exclusively to simultaneous action. (The notable exception here is Livy, whose Latin was sometimes mocked for its *Patavinitas*—its provincial imprecision.) Accordingly, the tenses of Greek and Latin participles, like the tenses of the infinitives, tend to be more tense-like, and less purely aspectual; but they are no longer about *absolute* time, but about time *relative to the time of the main verb.*

### *Supplementary participles*

The supplementary uses of the participle are in many ways the oddest of the lot. They are in a dynamic relationship with certain verbs or classes of verbs, and their use can't be considered attributive at all, nor can it be considered circumstantial. Supplementary uses of the participle fall into three subcategories:

1. After verbs of starting, stopping, or continuing
2. After verbs expressing a mental or emotional state, to provide its cause
3. After three other particular verbs: τυγχάνω, λανθάνω, and φθάνω

There are English constructions somewhat similar to the first two of these, though the English constructions are somewhat deceptive, since our versions are usually thought to engage the gerund rather than participle. These are the Greek versions:

> ἄρχεται λέγων.
> *He begins talking.*
>
> διατελέσουσι βαίνων.
> *They will continue walking.*
>
> ἔπαυσα φαγῶν.
> *I stopped eating.*

χαίρω πέσσων.

*I am happy [while/when] cooking.*

*(I.e., I enjoy cooking.)*

### Participles in indirect discourse

Participles are also used—in something that is similar to the supplementary use of the participle—in certain forms of indirect discourse (specifically indirect statement). We have discussed that much already.

**CHAPTER 10**

# Pronouns

*A word for all seasons*

If all signification is a kind of pointing, then the pronoun is arguably the most advanced and versatile of signifiers. Its intrinsic neutrality of meaning enables it to be assigned freely wherever one needs a shorter word for ease and clarity of discourse. It's called a pronoun from the Latin *pronomen*—and really all that means is that it stands in for a noun.

A pronoun gains its specific local significance by being attached (for the time being) to a given noun called its *antecedent.* And it's in that ability to acquire its meaning from its context that its glory and its weakness lie. Any given pronoun can be attached to one noun after another, like a strip of Velcro—attached, ripped off, attached to another, and so on, seemingly without limit. Like Velcro, however, it's also quite willing to adhere to any suitable medium fairly indiscriminately, whether it was what the author intended or not. It can pick up almost any other kind of fiber, fluff, or generic garbage. It's up to you to keep the pieces straight.

## A summary of the types of pronouns

Being a universally configurable pointer, the pronoun also highlights in the diversity of its forms the various ways in which such pointing can work. Here we have identified ten forms. I should also make it clear that I am following the ancient practice of referring to both pronouns and pronoun-like adjectives under the one umbrella term. If you're working with some grammars and some textbooks, their practice will correspond to this approach; in others, they will be separated into two classes where relevant. It won't really matter greatly which way you go, as long as you grasp the functional distinction between the two kinds, and the formal similarity between them. Figure 11 shows how the types of pronouns break down—including which are substantive and which are adjectival in function.

**Fig. 11.** Types of Pronouns

| Pronoun type | Functions as | |
|---|---|---|
| | Noun | Adjective |
| Personal | ■ | — |
| Demonstrative | ■ | ■ |
| Possessive | — | ■ |
| Reflexive | ■ | — |
| Reflexive Possessive | — | ■ |
| Reciprocal | ■ | — |
| Intensive | ■ | — |
| Interrogative | ■ | ■ |
| Indefinite | ■ | ■ |
| Relative | ■ | ■ |
| Correlative | ■ | ■ |

All these different forms of pronouns and adjectives function similarly, in that they stand in for nouns (substantive or adjective)—and all of them require an antecedent, express or implied, to complete their meaning. Within that range they have a spectacular array of abilities. In both Greek and Latin, some of these forms intersect. The idiomatic usage of pronouns is no trifling matter, and the nonnative speaker of almost any language is likelier to run aground with these than with almost any other kind of word.

## Personal pronouns

Personal pronouns are almost always the first things that come to mind when people talk of pronouns, and it's probably natural: they concern the place of the speaker and the addressee specifically and allow many sentences that (in English, at least) would be impossible otherwise. Personal pronouns, properly considered, are purely nominal in function: they do not have adjectival equivalents or uses.

Their function is less critical in Latin and Greek, where they are dominated by their oblique cases: in both Greek and Latin, the verb itself indicates the person and number of the subject. In the third person, that's sometimes sufficient; in the first and second, it's almost always enough. In Latin we can say:

> Romam ibam.
>
> *I was going to Rome.*

In the nominative, therefore, neither Latin nor Greek normally resorts to pronouns of the first or second person, unless there is a particular reason to emphasize it.

In the third person, neither Latin nor Greek actually *has* a normal nonreflexive personal pronoun (equivalent to our "he," "she," or "it"). To provide for those functions, the normal word to use is the demonstrative pronoun.

## Demonstrative pronouns

Demonstrative pronouns (from the Latin *demonstro, -are*, "point out") are sometimes called "deictic" by linguists (from the Greek δείκνυμι, which also means "point out"). Whichever term one prefers, they are among the most flexible of pronouns—sometimes maddeningly so. They slide very freely from the substantive to the adjective form and back again, as we noted above with the following pair:

> Where did you get that?
> Where did you get that hat?

When accompanied by a noun, the demonstrative is content to take an adjectival role, reinforcing or specifying the noun in question, usually differentiating it from other possible references: in the example, it would distinguish *that* hat (i.e., the one I'm pointing at now) from this hat or any other hat one might be thinking of. It will just as easily stand alone, without a noun, as long as all parties to the conversation understand the reference. If they do not, confusion (if not hilarity) may well ensue.

### Weak demonstratives

Latin and Greek demonstratives fall into two broad classes: some we call strong, and others we call weak, depending on the specificity with which they do their pointing out. The strong ones are much more closely bound to place; we'll talk shortly about what that entails. The weak ones are very much like the third-person personal pronoun in English, though they can still assume substantive or adjective forms, as personal pronouns, properly speaking, cannot. They function, therefore, much the way "he," "she," and "it" do in English, though they take their gender from grammatical gender rather than from the actual sex of the person or thing under discussion. (English is largely a genderless language, and so we use "he" or "she" to refer only to male or female persons or (occasionally, but not reliably) animals. Some English speakers will refer to a pet animal as "he" or "she," while others will use "it."

The Latin weak demonstrative is *is, ea, id*. In the nominative case, one is somewhat more likely to encounter it than the personal pronoun of the first or second person, but if the subject of a given sentence is adequately understood, it is still fairly likely to be omitted. The adjectival form is susceptible to a little more nuance, and there seems to be no hard and fast rule about when it must be applied, especially in the nominative. It functions adjectivally very much the way the definite article does in English: it flags the word to which it is attached as something that has already come up in the conversation, or else is immediately in view of the speaker.

> Is liber de re militari docet.

> *This/that/the book teaches about military business.*

Again, in the oblique cases, and when used as a substantive, it has somewhat more to do: it functions much as a third-person personal pronoun might, and is probably most reliably understood as being the equivalent of "he," "she," or "it":

> Cum Catilinae epistulas lexisset, Cicero **eum** denuntiavit.

> *When he had read Catiline's letters, Cicero denounced* **him**.

> Valde Philippicis orationibus Ciceronis iratus, Antonius **ei** nullomodo parcere voluit.

> *Having been greatly angered by Cicero's Philippic orations, Antony was not at all willing to spare* **him**.

The Greek equivalent is not so simple: it engages the delightfully protean word αὐτός, which is capable of being used in three distinct ways: as a substantive demonstrative pronoun, as an adjective in the attributive position (nestled between the article and the noun), and as an adjective in the predicative position (anywhere other than the attributive position). Like the Latin weak demonstrative, the last of these tends not to appear in the nominative very much, except as an intensifier. A few examples will have to suffice, but they should give a sense of how very flexible (and useful) all three of these are. Consider:

ὅτε τῷ Σωκράτη ἐγίγνετο υἱός, ἐπαίδευσε **αὐτόν**.

*When a son was born to Socrates, he educated **him**.*

Here, the demonstrative αὐτόν is being used as a simple personal pronoun—it is the accusative direct object of ἐπαίδευσε—"educated." Now consider this example:

**αὐτὸς** ἐπαίδευσε ὁ Σωκράτης τὸν υἱόν.

*Socrates **himself** educated his [the] son.*

Here, the nominative αὐτός, standing in predicative position, is used to reinforce the subject as an emphatic form, meaning "himself," and hence is not here considered a demonstrative, but an intensive pronoun. These will be discussed below, but it seems useful to see the range of the same word in action here. In attributive position, it acquires the lexical sense of "the same":

ὁ Σωκράτης ἐπαίδευσε τὸν **αὐτὸν** υἱόν.

*Socrates educated **the same** son.*

These can be combined in the same sentence to occasionally startling effect:

**αὐτὸς** ὁ Σωκράτης τὸν **αὐτὸν** υἱὸν ἐπαίδευσε.

*Socrates himself educated the **same** son.*

Only the first of these three is strictly demonstrative, but the case of αὐτός should be sufficient to show that the boundaries between these classes of pronoun are at least somewhat porous.

### Another use for the definite article

Greek has one more effective demonstrative to conjure from its bag of tricks, and this is its occasional use of the definite article as a kind of weak demonstrative. Historically, this is entirely reasonable, because the definite article is apparently a weakened demonstrative in the first place: in Homer and other very early Greek, one can find it used as a real demonstrative.

Of all the pronouns in Greek, it is the most likely to perplex students, precisely because it crops up without warning, and it looks like something else. This doesn't happen with Latin at all, of course, because Latin has no article to treat this way. In Attic and later Greek, it usually arises only in situations where the author is contrasting two things. Any student of Greek will have encountered the particles μέν and δέ (which are usually laboriously translated as "on the one hand" and "on the other hand," at least until the student acquires a more native feel for the language). These two particles are typically used to set off balanced phrases, clauses, or sentences that are opposed in some way, which accounts for the more mechanical translation. When combined with the article alone, however, a certain transformation happens, as if by magic, and the articles begin to function as pronouns, without ever being attached to a noun, to mean (in the singular) "the one" and "the other," or (in the plural) "some" and "others." Students seeing this for the first few (or few dozen) times will often panic, thinking that they have somehow mislaid the noun to which the article should attach, but it's not the case. This is most common in Attic prose, and won't show up in Homer or (for the most part) dramatic Attic. For example,

> τοὺς μὲν ἀπέκτεινε, τοὺς δ᾽ ἐξέβαλεν
>
> *Some he put to death; others he expelled.*
>
> —Xenophon, *Anabasis* 1.1.7

If the reference is indefinite, the indefinite pronoun τις or one of its forms may be added for clarification:

> οἱ μέν τινες αὐτοῖς πελάσαντες ταχὺ ἀπέθνησκον, οἱ δ᾽ ἔφευγον, οἱ δέ τινες καὶ ἑάλωσαν αὐτῶν . . .
>
> *Some, having approached them, were killed at once, while others fled, and some others of them were captured . . .*
>
> Xenophon, *The Education of Cyrus* 3.2.10

### Strong demonstratives

Strong demonstratives are not, as words, any stronger than the so-called weak demonstratives; nor are they strong in the sense that strong verbs are strong—that is, exhibiting basic vowel changes in their stems. They are called "strong" merely because they point out their objects with greater specificity than the weak demonstratives.

In English we have two demonstrative pronouns, "this" and "that." The scope of these can vary a good deal; "this" can refer to something in the immediate vicinity of the speaker, but it can be within a two-foot radius of the speaker or it can be the overall condition of the world in which the speaker finds himself or herself. "That" is, by contrast, something separated, physically or conceptually, from the speaker in some way. It can be relatively near or very far. As with almost everything involved in language, context is the great determiner of what's what. If you have your index finger on a map of the Milky Way, you might say:

> This star is Alpha Centauri.

Obviously Alpha Centauri itself is not terribly close to you (just as well, really); nor is it necessarily even any closer to you than other depictions or representations of stars on the map. The word "this" is justified chiefly because you are making contact with the map and associating yourself with the reference.

Latin and Greek each have three pronouns that are normally considered "strong." In Latin they are *hic, iste,* and *ille,* normally translated as "this," "that," and "that [over there]." In Greek the alignment is virtually identical: the words are ὅδε, οὗτος, and ἐκεῖνος. For most speakers of English, the distinction between "this" and "that" is not at all difficult to rationalize and understand. The more complex nuance comes in distinguishing the two kinds of "that" or "that over there." Often the difference between the two is represented as one of relative proximity: "that" referring to something not terribly far away as opposed to "that over there; yonder." That distinction is basically correct, but the difference between them can probably be best understood under a rubric we don't normally apply to pronouns that are more or less definitionally of the third person already—namely, that of person.

## "Persons" of the strong demonstratives

As noted, the demonstrative pronouns are all functionally third-person pronouns. While one can theoretically refer to oneself with "this," it's usually casual or slangy. In P.D.Q. Bach's immortal opera *The Abduction of Figaro,* Dona Donna tells her erstwhile lover Donald Giovanni:

> This is one dame you'll never leave again.

But it's not the norm. Usually one uses "this" to refer to something else within reach or close to the speaker. In Greek drama, at least, forms of ὅδε can be used similarly to refer to the speaker:

> τῆσδε γε ζώσες ἔτι
> *This one [I] still living (genitive absolute)*
> *(I.e., While I am yet alive)*
>
> —Sophocles, *The Women of Trachis* 305

Similarly the forms of οὗτος can be used for the second person—that is, "you":

τίς οὑτοσί;

*Who is this?*

*(I.e., Who are you?)*

—Aristophanes, The Acharnians 1048

The interesting fact is that the three strong demonstratives exhibit a remarkable correlation with the three grammatical persons, and keeping track of this and how it works can help in understanding the actual domains and connotations of all three.

Like English "this," Latin *hic* and Greek ὅδε correspond to whatever is within reach of, or in the general surroundings (perceived or conceived) of, the speaker. These pronouns are sometimes called *demonstratives of the first person*. This is the simple case, though it's important that you remember that this doesn't mean that they are necessarily first-person *forms*. They are not.

English has only one other demonstrative pronoun, "that" (and its plural "those"), which refers to anything that is *not* in the personal range or area of the speaker. Latin and Greek, however, have two, and probably the best way to understand them is to see them as representing the other two grammatical persons. *Iste* in Latin and οὗτος in Greek are not merely closer to the speaker than the more distant *ille* and ἐκεῖνος, but they are more closely associated with the context or domain of the addressee. *Iste* refers to what is not just somewhere between right here and away over yonder, but something that is *there with you*. Both are sometimes referred to in grammar texts as *demonstratives of the second person*. This conveys an important idea, but again it must be emphasized that they are not actually second-person forms; they are still third. That is, they are not referring to the addressee in any respect other than localization.

Latin *ille* and Greek ἐκεῖνος, finally, are really "over there"—away from both the speaker and the addressee. They designate a separate and more objectively remote space. Sometimes (unsurprisingly at this point) these pronouns are referred to as *demonstratives of the third person*. This has nothing to do with their being third-person pronouns as such—though they are nevertheless.

One conundrum this distribution helps to explain is the fact that Greek οὗτος and (especially) Latin *iste* often have a pejorative sense. I would suggest that *iste* is in fact a fairly morally neutral word in and of itself; it takes on a contemptuous tone chiefly when referring to a person. Imaginatively reconstructing the kind of situation in which this comes into play, however, should not be difficult. If I am talking to you about someone else who is far off, referring to him or her using the third person in your presence has no negative connotations. But if I begin talking about someone who is *with* you—someone either intentionally in your company, or at least in your immediate vicinity (close enough that he or she can hear the conversation)—while all the time referring to him or her in the third person, as if talking *around* but not *to* him or her, that inevitably seems rude or contemptuous. I suspect most, if not all, such pejorative or contemptuous usages of the word come from this perspective.

Cicero uses *iste* to refer to Catiline in his speeches to the Senate, but when he does so, he is not *addressing* Catiline. When he is addressing Catiline, he says:

> Quam diu etiam furor iste tuus nos eludet?
>
> *How long will that frenzy of yours escape our notice?*
>
> —Cicero, *Against Catiline* 1.1

The use of *iste* here, I would argue, does not particularly indicate that Cicero has contempt for Catiline (though he does): it's because it's referring to that *furor* with or in the vicinity of Catiline, to whom he is speaking. Later in the same passage, Cicero does indeed refer to Catiline himself as *iste*—and that arguably *is* pejorative, because he is talking *about* Catiline, although he is present to the rest of the Senate.

In Greek, the picture is similar, but somewhat more complicated, and capable of greater nuance. Normally ὅδε will refer to someone immediately present and significantly highlighted; οὗτος refers to someone either not so immediately present or someone less important than the person denoted by ὅδε. The arrival of a new character or speaker in Attic drama is normally announced with ὅδε. The full range of possibilities here is beyond the scope of this book, but more detail can be extracted from Smyth §§1238ff.

## Here and there in time

The two extremes of the person polarity—that is, the demonstratives of the first and third persons—also have a sense of proximity in *time*. *Hic* in Latin normally will refer to the thing closest to the time of speaking, and *ille* to the one that's more remote. Accordingly, if two things have been mentioned already in the discourse, *hic* will normally refer to the latter—the thing that is more recent, or temporally closer. *Ille* refers to the former—the one that is farther off in the past.

In Greek, these rules are a bit less reliable. Generally, ὅδε refers to what immediately *follows* in the conversation. Most commonly, too, οὗτος will refer to what has immediately *preceded* in the conversation, though it can in some situations refer to something following as well. Ἐκεῖνος, however, will almost always refer to something preceding—and if there are several things, to the more remote of them: that is, "the former," like Latin *ille*.

It's beyond the scope here to delve into all the nuances of the demonstratives in Greek or Latin. Smyth (§§1238–61) has considerable discussion about the variations in Greek usage in particular, which are quite complex. Sometimes demonstratives will be combined in quite unexpected ways, such as ὅδε ἐκεῖνος—which may startle the novice, but is not intuitively wrong, once one sees how the whole phrase works:

ὅδ᾽ ἐκεῖνος ἐγώ

*I here [am] that one.*

*(I.e., I'm the one we've been talking about.)*

—Sophocles, *Oedipus at Colonus* 138

Obviously this does not literally mean that I here am that one over there; what it *does* mean is that the subject of discussion, hitherto treated as remote, is being identified with the speaker. As such, it's not far off from the English usage:

Thou speak'st aright;
I am that merry wanderer of the night.

—William Shakespeare, *A Midsummer Night's Dream* 2.1.43

## Possessive pronouns

The possessive pronoun or adjective is purely adjectival in its basic form, but (like most adjectives) it can be substantivized. The English examples are "my," "our," "your," "his," "her," "its," and "their." In Greek and Latin they are well-behaved adjectives of a fairly standard form, derived from the personal pronoun, though sometimes their morphology varies. In any case, they naturally assume the gender, case, and number of the noun to which they are attached, whether that noun is explicit or not (in the case of substantivization). They can sometimes create confusion for English speakers, since, because they agree with the nouns they modify, they do *not* necessarily take the gender, case, or number of the person or thing doing the possessing (unlike the genitive *eius* of the weak demonstrative). A handful of examples will suffice to convey the general idea. Thus:

Haec ornamenta sunt mea.

*These are my jewels; these jewels are mine.*

—Valerius Maximus 4.4

When substantivized, they can refer to the relevant things already under discussion: when the context has not been specified, usually the reference is to people. Hence:

Pauci de nostris cadunt.

*A few of/from our [number, people] fall. (historical present: understand "fell")*

—Caesar, Gallic War 1.15

This latter usage sometimes produces confusion among beginning students, but it seldom offers any real conceptual difficulty when the context and meaning are understood.

Possession is often left unexpressed in both Latin and Greek, when the context leaves no real doubt about the referent. Any idiomatic understanding of

Socrates filios edocuit.

Σωκράτης τοὺς υἱοὺς ἐπαίδευσε.

*Socrates taught the sons.*

would imply that the sons Socrates taught were his own. This is true in the case of almost all relational terms. If Socrates were teaching someone else's sons, that would require specific mention.

In Latin, when possession does need to be made explicit, however, there is a choice to make. If the possessor is the subject of the sentence (or, sometimes, just of the clause that contains it), one will normally use the *reflexive* possessive adjective, discussed below, which exists in all three persons.

Where the possessor is someone other than the subject, however, the situation becomes a little more complicated. For the first or second person, we will still use the possessive adjective, which looks exactly like the reflexive possessive adjective. One wouldn't use the genitive of the personal pronoun, as does sometimes happen in Greek or (irregularly) in English. A native speaker of Latin would doubtless have understood such a solecism—there's really no other way to construe it—but it would probably sound as bizarre to his or her ears as "me's hat" or "that hat is of me" would to a native English-speaker, as a way to convey the idea "my hat" or "that hat is mine."

For the third person, however, there are no nonreflexive possessive adjectives available. (This is probably to be expected, since the possessive adjectives mirror the personal pronouns, and there are no third-person forms of those either.) When dealing with the third person, therefore, Latin normally resorts to the genitive of the weak demonstrative *is*, *ea*, *id*, which, as was discussed above, serves as the third-person personal pronoun—hence *eius* (all genders in the singular), *eorum* (masculine or neuter plural), or *earum* (feminine plural) serves for all practical purposes as the nonreflexive third-person possessive adjective.

The possessive adjective/pronoun in Greek functions similarly, though there are somewhat more possibilities for irregularity. In a practical sense, it's much like Latin, since only forms for the first and second persons, corresponding to the personal pronouns of the first and second persons, are in common usage. (Historically, this is not true: there was a third-person possessive pronoun ὅς, ἥ, ὅν, which appears in Homer, but not in Attic prose; the plural version, σφέτερος, -α, -ον, does survive into Attic, however.) Where Greek differs most sharply from Latin, however, is in allowing the use of the genitive of the personal pronoun as a kind of substitute for the possessive pronoun, even where that form would be perfectly comfortable. Semantically, the two are virtually identical; syntactically, however, one is a substantive, and the other is an adjective. In the third-person singular, the only nonreflexive option in Attic Greek is to use the relevant genitive of αὐτός—αὐτοῦ (masculine and neuter) or αὐτῆς (feminine) for the singular; αὐτῶν (all genders) is used in Attic at least as frequently as σφέτερος, -α, -ον for the plural.

Accordingly one can have

> ὁ ἐμὸς ξῖφος
> *my sword*

or

> ὁ ἐμοῦ ξῖφος
> *[the] of me [masc.] sword*
> *(I.e., my sword [if the speaker is a man])*

or

> ὁ ἐμῆς ξίφος
> *[the] of me [fem.] sword*
> *(I.e., my sword [if the speaker is a woman])*

# Reflexive personal pronouns

The idea of reflexivity changes some of the ground rules in both Greek and Latin, as it does also to some extent in English. We are not perhaps accustomed to think of the problem thoroughly (or clearly) as native speakers, partly because the usage seems obvious to us, but also because we use the same form for our reflexive and intensive pronouns (which will be discussed below). This muddies the waters considerably even for intermediate students. If it's any consolation, the Greeks and especially the Romans and their successors were a little foggy on some of this too: mismanagement of the reflexive pronouns was endemic to Late and Vulgar Latin.

The English reflexive pronoun is "myself," "yourself," "himself," "herself," and "itself" in the singular, and "ourselves," "yourselves," and "themselves" (for all genders) in the third-person plural. (Why the forms are not "hisself" or "their-selves" on the one hand, or "meself" or "youself" on the other, is a matter of some historical complexity, and even native speakers of English, especially those who have not been diligently schooled, often make mistakes with these, usually of the form "hisself" or "theirselves." English is a tangled historical mess of a language.)

The point of the reflexive pronoun is that it represents specifically and exclusively the person or thing that is the subject of the sentence in some *other* role or function in the sentence. It's called "reflexive" because it "bends back" (*reflectere*—the root of our word "reflect," as well as "reflex") on the subject. These are special-use personal pronouns: like the other personal pronouns, they are always substantive in sense, and never adjectival.

The chief implication of this fact is that the reflexive pronouns, though they are present in all three persons, never occur in the nominative. This strikes some people as arbitrary at first, but it isn't: it's organic to the meaning of the reflexive pronoun, and there could never be a possible nominative use for it.

In English, therefore, we can see the subject represented reflexively with such formulations as the following:

> I hit myself with the hammer.
> I gave [to] myself a present.
> I am telling you about myself.

In Latin, the reflexive pronouns are in form identical to the personal pronoun in the first and second persons throughout, and it's probably of purely academic interest to distinguish the two. We say that they're reflexive pronouns if they refer to the subject, and normal (nonreflexive) personal pronouns if they don't.

It's really only in the third person that they show up with distinctively different forms, which are based on the *s*- root. In a characteristic burst of Roman linguistic economy, the plural and singular forms are identical, too; this never creates any ambiguity, because the number of the subject is already established by and in the subject. Between the collapse of both numbers into one, and the elimination of the nominative as logically impossible, we are left with only four forms: *sui*, *sibi*, *se*, and *se*. The last two of those are the same in form as well, though in any given situation it will be either accusative or ablative.

Part of the glory of the Latin reflexive is that it is different from any other pronouns in form. Strictly, it should refer back only to the subject of the sentence, though in some cases we find that an author—even a "good" classical author—will lose track of the subject and the main clause, and accordingly drop in a *sibi* or a *se* that refers to the subject of a subordinate clause. One can cluck and fret about such things, but they accord with and express the author's understanding of what is really dominating the sentence: when this happens, we can assume that he has come to regard this secondary subject as the main focus of his attention.

The Greek reflexive pronouns are more tangled. They are formed by fusing the stem of the personal pronoun with the relevant (but again only oblique) forms of αὐτός. In the singular, these are normally written as one word: ἐμαυτοῦ, ἐμαυτης, and so on; σεαυτοῦ, σεαυτῆς, and so on; ἑαυτοῦ, ἑαυτῆς, and so on. In the plural, for no particular reason that I have been able to determine, the parts are normally kept separate: ἡμῶν αὐτῶν, ἡμῖν αὐτοῖς, and so on; ὑμῶν αὐτῶν, ὑμῖν αὐτοῖς, and so on. Lest it all be too predictable, Greek does allow for two different variations in the third-person plural: either ἑαυτῶν (in keeping with the singular) or σφῶν αὐτῶν, ἑαυτοῖς / -αῖς, or σφίσιν αὐτοῖς / -αῖς, and so on.

## Reflexive possessive adjectives

Reflexive possessive adjectives are a Latin phenomenon. Greek doesn't have them, and English doesn't have them, unless one wants to argue that the appended "own" creates a new form in sentences like this:

> When he was visiting his wealthy friend, he took his own car to the store.

Unlike the reflexive *personal* pronouns in the foregoing section, but like other possessive pronouns, reflexive possessive pronouns are entirely adjectival (though it needs to be pointed out that, like any other adjective, they are capable of being substantivized). The reflexive possessive is the same for all genders of possessor, but, like any other adjective (and like the possessives discussed above), it can take a full range of gender, number, and case endings to agree with whatever word it is modifying (the thing possessed).

Given what has already been said about reflexive pronouns, it's probably unsurprising that what distinguishes the reflexive possessive pronoun is the fact that it refers back to a possessor that is the subject of the sentence. Compare

> Catullus Cornelio de poematis suis [reflexive] scripsit.
>
> *Catullus wrote to Cornelius concerning his [own; i.e., Catullus's] poems.*

and

> Catullus Calvo de poematis eius [not reflexive] scripsit.
>
> *Catullus wrote to Calvus concerning his [Calvus's] poems.*

Almost any Latin speaker of the classical era would have understood the distinction intuitively and completely. It's worth noting that even in "good" authors, occasionally a reflexive adjective will refer to the more prominent entity in the sentence even if it is not the subject:

> Hunc sui cives a civitate ejecerunt.
>
> *His [own] citizens threw him [Hannibal] out of the city.*
>
> —Cicero, *In Defense of Sestius* 68

This deviation from the standard is almost certainly aided by the fact that *hunc* is particularly prominent because it's the first word of the sentence.

## Reciprocal pronouns

Latin has a reflexive possessive pronoun whereas Greek does not; Greek returns the favor by having one of the most elegantly specialized pronoun forms out there—namely, the reciprocal pronoun. This is a kind of permutation of the personal pronoun, and hence it's once again substantive rather than an adjective. Its sense is "each other." We can express that synthetically in English, but Greek has a single inflected form to take care of it—namely, ἀλλήλων. When required to convey the same sense, Latin resorts typically to the reflexive (*se* or sometimes *inter se*), leaving some potential for confusion.

The reciprocal pronoun shares certain characteristics with the reflexive pronoun, too. Like the reflexive, it has no nominative form—there is no rational semantic situation that would require it. It is further constrained (again, on reasonable semantic grounds) to the dual and plural numbers. One of anything cannot do anything to each other: the idea doesn't make sense. Here Xenophon uses the reciprocal pronoun quite conventionally:

> ὡς δ᾽ εἰδέτην ἀλλήλους ἡ γυνὴ καὶ ὁ Ἀβραδάτας, ἠσπάζοντο ἀλλήλους . . .
>
> *When Abradatas and his wife saw one another, they embraced each other . . .*
>
> —Xenophon, *The Education of Cyrus* 6.1.47

## Intensive pronouns

Intensive pronouns in English are often difficult for beginning students to distinguish from the reflexive, since they take the same form—"himself," "herself," "itself," and "themselves." Their functions are entirely distinct, but in fact there seems to be a long heritage of confusing or conflating them in multiple languages—not just in English. In Greek, of course, since the reflexive is already naturally a compound built with some form of αὐτός, the potential for confusion is fairly close to the surface. In Latin, although the forms are distinct, that doesn't prevent them from being at least partly fused or intermixed. Especially when an author wants to emphasize the reflexivity of the pronoun, it is not uncommon to see *seipsum*, or (even more emphatic, with the infix *-met-*) *semetipsum* or the like. These forms spread like aggressive garden weeds into the Romance languages, yielding standard intensive forms like French *même* and Spanish *mismo*.

Arguably the intensive pronoun accomplishes no essential function in the semantic makeup of a sentence; it adds only an emphasis (often because the identification is seen as somehow surprising or contrary to expectation). In English we have such things as

> I myself built this house.

in which "myself" merely reinforces the unexpectedness or exceptional quality of the subject, and

> I did that myself.

in which the "myself" is at least semantically part of what the sentence is trying to say.

The Latin and Greek usages are more or less similar, though in Greek the use of αὐτός (in the predicative, not the attributive position) has its own range of nuances, some of them quite elegant in their expressive power.

## Interrogative pronouns and adjectives

Interrogative pronouns and adjectives are in a way the exception to the general rule concerning pronouns and pronominal adjectives—namely, that the referent needs to be supplied reliably before the pronoun is used. Interrogative pronouns are used precisely because the referent is *not* clear; they are seeking clarification on this point:

> Who built the house?
> To whom did you give the car keys?

Both exemplify the interrogative pronoun.

Interrogatives also have both substantive and adjectival forms. One can plausibly ask:

> Who built this house?

in which case "who" is fully substantive. One can as easily ask:

> What/which contractor built this house?

Here the "what" or "which" is modifying "contractor"—assuming that it was a contractor rather than a butcher or a baker, but expressing the uncertainty of the speaker about which of many possible contractors might have been involved. As noted, the form of the word chosen may well vary between substantive and adjective uses; we would not normally say:

> What built this house?

or

> Who contractor built this house?

So it is also in Latin and (less frequently) in Greek. In Latin, "who" in a substantive sense is *quis*, while adjectivally it would be the interrogative adjective (adjectival pronoun) that properly agrees with the substantive. Hence:

> Quis aedificium erexit?
> *Who built [the] building?*

but

> Qui homo aedificium erexit?
>
> *What person built [the] building?*

The form *quis* represents men and women indifferently; the neuter form *quid* is reserved for inanimate things, even if the noun that emerges as an answer to the question is masculine or feminine. Thus:

> Quid est?
>
> *What is it?*

but

> Quae res est?
>
> *What thing is it?*

The Latin interrogative adjective agrees, as noted, with whatever noun it is modifying; its forms are identical to the forms of the relative pronoun. The two cannot be distinguished purely by form, then, but only by context. Seldom, in a rationally punctuated modern text, is there any likelihood of confusion between them; in manuscripts such confusions can occasionally arise.

The Greek interrogative pronoun, on the other hand, shares its forms not with the relative, but with the *indefinite* pronoun, which we will discuss below. Here it usually *is* possible to distinguish the one from the other merely by appearance, however, because the interrogative is always accented (and an acute accent never changes to a grave, even though it would otherwise do so), while the indefinite is enclitic, which means that it "throws" its accent back on the preceding word, and so usually is not carrying one of its own. In some situations, because of an accumulation of enclitics, the indefinite pronoun may wind up wearing a borrowed hat, so to speak, from the word following it. Here again, context and a careful regard for the actual meaning of the text are the solution to the problem. Because the adjectival indefinite is virtually always attached to the end of the word it refers to, and it agrees with it in case, number, and gender, there is fairly little chance of real confusion.

Greek interrogative τίς is etymologically related to Latin *quis*, reflecting certain sound changes in initial consonants. For the most part, the adjectival and substantive forms are identical; hence:

> τίς ἐστι;
>
> *Who is it?*

and

> τίς ἄνθρωπός ἐστι;
>
> *What person is it?*

As with Latin, the adjectival form will agree with the noun it refers to, but if used substantively it will follow the distinction between persons and things:

> τί ἐστι;
>
> *What is it?*

but

> τίς ξῖφός ἐστι;
>
> *What sword is it?*

## Indefinite pronouns

The indefinite pronoun serves the function of the English indefinite article or some other modifier like "a certain . . ." English doesn't have such things, perhaps because it has an indefinite article. Latin accomplishes the same thing with an adjectival modifier (sometimes substantivized without anything to stand for it). It is in Greek that these things truly come into their own. In Greek, the forms of the indefinite pronoun are the same as those of the interrogative pronoun (to which they may be causally related), except for the fact that they are enclitic. This is consistent with the fact that the indefinite follows the word modified. Accordingly,

> ἄνθρωπός τις

is equivalent to Latin

> homo quidam

or English

> *a certain person*

There's not really a lot more to be said about indefinite pronouns: they are fairly tame, and act in highly predictable ways. They seldom connect to anything else other than insofar as they specify that the word modified (which may be in the nominative or any other case) is not someone we should know already, or something that has appeared hitherto in the discourse.

# Relative pronouns

Relative pronouns are the pivot on which the relative clause attaches to its parent. We have already discussed relative clauses above: they are adjectival in function, and the relative pronoun represents in the relative clause (usually as a substantive) the word that is its antecedent.

As noted earlier, there has been a great deal too much bother made concerning the relative pronoun: its apparently divided loyalties are not really divided at all. For all that, the range of its possibilities is exceptionally large: the adjectival relative clause is a powerhouse of signification.

# Correlative pronouns

Smyth's *Greek Grammar* (§340) has an especially illuminating chart showing how many of the Greek pronouns (pronominal adjectives, in particular) are correlated; once you see the chart, it's fairly clear how they relate to one another. There's probably not a lot of use in reproducing it here or belaboring its contents other than to note that Greek correlative pronouns tend to be related to one another very systematically, and to share a certain parallelism of form. There are Latin correlatives too; one can probably pick up most of what needs to be known about them by looking at Allen and Greenough §152, which presents a very similar chart for Latin.

# CHAPTER 11

# Other Little Words

*The little bits and pieces that grease the wheels*

There are a number of other little words of one sort or another that add flavor and direction to sentences. They fall broadly into two classes: those that are somehow relevant to the "flow of traffic" in a clause or sentence, though without much intrinsic meaning of their own—syntactic glue, as I called them above—and others that are instead added to a sentence to provide it with flavor and nuances of meaning, but which have relatively little control function. Those familiar with computer programming may find it useful to consider that the former class comprises chiefly words marking program control ("if," "then," "while," etc.), while the latter class contains mostly things that would never appear in a programming language at all. Most of the semantic meaning of a sentence is conveyed by the more specific words: nouns (variables and constants) and verbs (function and procedure calls), with the frugal admixture of various modifiers.

## Articles

The article is a curious little word, since it's not strictly necessary in all places. English has an article—two of them, in fact: the definite article "the" (cognate with German *der, die, das*) and the indefinite article "a" or "an" (semantically and syntactically equivalent, but adjusted for euphony before vowels and consonants). Articles are only ever used to modify nouns (either substantives or substantivized adjectives). They are in a broader sense members of the elusive class of quantifiers—indeed, both "a" and "an" are derived from Old English *ān*, meaning "one"— cognate with German *ein*.

The difference between the definite and the indefinite article has to do with the cloudy domain of discourse management: we tend to use "the" when we expect that the hearer will know what is meant by the noun in question, and "a" when we do not, or when distinguishing a particular referent is of no importance. Often the presumption of knowledge is based on the fact that we have talked about the thing earlier in the same conversation—in such cases, "the" (without any further modifiers) is used to flag the noun as "the one we were talking about just now"—but it can also be used when the referent is presumed to be clear. We do not have to have been talking about the president of the United States or the Federal Reserve Board to use "the" with either: it's presumed that the hearer knows which president of the United States or which Federal Reserve Board we're talking about. Articles can apply to either proper names or improper ones. We do not, however, tend to use the article with personal names unless we intend to make a distinction among several persons with the same name. If we are eager to distinguish John Adams the second president from another John Adams who runs an automobile repair shop in Poughkeepsie, we might say, "*the* John Adams who was president." Otherwise, we use personal names without articles, and the same goes for names of companies or other organizations like Apple or Microsoft. Where the name is specifically descriptive, however, and we want to make sure that it is clear that we are referring to the one that bears the description as a name, we will still use "the," as in "the United Nations" and so on. The nuances of managing articles comes as second nature to native speakers, but can cause no end of difficulty to those first learning the language.

Greek has a very powerful definite article, ὁ, ἡ, τό, but no indefinite article. The sense of the indefinite article can be rendered by adding the indefinite pronoun τις, discussed in the previous chapter. The definite article, however, is used very extensively, and (unlike English) Greek *will* normally use it with a proper name, again to verify that the person under discussion is the one you were thinking about already. Hence Greek will refer to

> ὁ Σωκράτης
>
> *Socrates*

or

> τὸ καλόν
>
> *the Good (either the ideal of goodness or [all] that which is good)*

Latin has no article, and seems to get along just fine without it, but it is worth noting that all the modern languages that have derived from Latin have picked up an article along the way. That article, moreover, is generally an outgrowth of a form of the (adjectival) demonstrative pronoun, and that makes a certain amount of sense, too. This derivation has occurred at various times throughout history in different languages. The Greek article has a particularly strong demonstrative force in Homeric Greek, and it is still in classical times capable (as noted in the discussion of pronouns) of functioning as a kind of weak demonstrative, given only a little support with things like the particles μέν and δέ. The Greek article also serves as a semantic delimiter, defining the space in which attributive, as opposed to predicative, adjectives may be placed: they always fall between the article and the noun. Hence:

> ὁ ἀγαθὸς ἄνθρωπος
>
> *the good person*

but

> ἀγαθὸς ὁ ἄνθρωπος.
>
> *The person is good.*

When this becomes unmanageable, or simply for the sake of variation, an attributive adjective can also follow a *repetition* of the article after the noun in question:

> ὁ ἄνθρωπος ὁ ἀγαθός
>
> *the good person*

It may be useful to think of the attributive position as a kind of "pocket" into which to put attributive adjectives; those adjectives that don't fall in the space so defined are different in intention and meaning.

The articles in the Romance languages similarly all appear to have derived—far later than the origin of the Greek article—from a truncation of various forms of *ille*, *illa, illud*, which are, as we discussed, the most remote of the strong demonstrative pronouns (the so-called demonstrative of the third person); this gives us Spanish *el, la*; French *le, la*; Italian *il, la*, and so on. Most of the Romance languages have systematically banished the neuter gender, leaving only the masculine and feminine.

## Particles

Most languages have words that could be considered particles, some of which are interjections; the rampant but nonspecific modern use of "like" might well be considered a particle of sorts. The word "to" used to form infinitives in English is generally considered a particle, as is "not," which is a negation particle. Some scholars cast a wider net, and consider a number of adverbs to be particles; this may or may not be useful, but I doubt that it's particularly critical one way or the other to the student of classical languages.

We chiefly talk about particles with respect to Greek—they are words that provide a certain flavor to sentences, and for the most part they would be hard to reduce to any single category, or to classify as any other normal part of speech. A professor I had in graduate school preferred to translate the emphatic participle δή by thumping the table at the appropriate point; what he did when he was without a table, I don't recall. Others, like μέν and δέ (often learned in the first weeks of Greek as "on the one hand" and "on the other hand," and unlearned over subsequent years), show (and convey to the hearer) the speaker's sense of the balance or opposition of the members of a sentence. Their actual denotation is slight, and their connotation, while powerful, is nebulous, and varies enormously with context. The particle ἄν has yet to be translated successfully, but it fundamentally changes any clause it appears in. It provides a note of unreality or contingency to its clause, such that it is used to mark the apodosis (the "then" portion, or the main clause) of a contrary-to-fact condition. All in all, there is no single simple way of translating or categorizing them all, and even the term "particle" here is a bit of a dodge: it refers to these little words as a kind of catchall term. Most of them in reality have a quasi-adverbial force, but the range of that force is enormous. As mentioned in chapter 1, particles are the subject of an entire learned book by J. D. Denniston called *The Greek Particles*, and it's curiously entertaining reading if you are of a suitable disposition.

There are particles in virtually all languages; we can talk about the particles of Latin or English or any other language as well.

## Prepositions

We talked above about how the preposition is ultimately an ossified sort of adverb, and how some (but not all) prepositions can still be used in an adverbial sense without an object. One might reasonably suppose, therefore, that prepositional phrases are always adverbial in their import. Usually, they are. They can, however, occur in places we would normally allocate to adjectives, with a clearly adjectival force:

> τεκμήριον μὲν τῆς **πρὸς ὑμᾶς** εὐνοίας, σημεῖον δὲ τῆς **πρὸς** Ἱππόνικον συνηθείας . . .
>
> *in proof of the **toward-you** goodwill and as a sign of the **toward-Hipponicus** friendship . . .*
>
> *(I.e., in proof of my goodwill **toward you** and in token of my friendship **for Hipponicus** . . . )*
>
> —Isocrates, *To Demonicus* 2

By extension of that same principle, prepositions can be substantivized, if appearing with an article, and can stand for a subject or an object:

τοὺς ὑπὸ χθονός

*those under the ground*

—Sophocles, *Antigone* 65

The other fact to remember about prepositions is that they take shape with respect to objects, and those objects are normally in a particular case. All that has been discussed under the heading of nouns above. There's fairly little to say about them beyond this that will be particularly surprising or illuminating, however.

## Conjunctions

Conjunctions fall into two general families—the coordinating conjunctions and the subordinating conjunctions. Coordinating conjunctions are those that attach two things at the same level of discourse. Subordinating conjunctions are those that attach dependent pieces—usually dependent clauses—to the clauses on which they depend.

Coordinating conjunctions in English are fairly few: we have "and" and "but," along with "for," "or," "nor," "yet," and "so"—the last of these being somewhat more adverbial than some would prefer for their conjunctions. "And" and "but" are the real critical players: the former introduces one thing that is parallel to another or in the same sequence, while the latter introduces something that is understood to be contrary or concessive in force. We can use them to join nouns, adjectives, verbs, or adverbs, or to connect whole clauses:

The shoes and the hat did not go together. (nouns)
The team was small but powerful. (adjectives)
The young girl skipped and danced down the street. (verbs)
Houdini escaped quickly but not easily. (adverbs)
We went to the store and we bought a fossilized goose. (clauses)
Tom ate fish, but Bill preferred steak. (clauses)

Subordinating conjunctions, on the other hand, are the fasteners that make possible any kind of complex sentence: the subordinating conjunction typically indicates what kind of clause is coming, and hence it tends to appear first in the clause, or very near the beginning. The range of subordinating conjunctions in any language is, for the same reason, significantly larger than that of coordinating conjunctions, but it's still a very small set. "When," "until," "though," "if," and the like all fall under this broad heading, and the kinds of clauses they introduce have been discussed above under adverbial clauses.

## Interjections

Interjections are effectively syntactically null—they are cut off from any explicit connection to the clauses in which they appear (if they do indeed appear in clauses; one can reasonably analyze them as standing outside the clausal structure altogether). Alternatively (and consistent with the name "interjection"), one can see them as something "thrown in" rather than properly attached to the clauses in which they appear. In the sentence

Wow, you sure don't look as if you had just run a ten-mile race.

it is really impossible to construe the "Wow" as a part of either the subject or the predicate: it simply "floats" over the sentence, much as certain particles do, to lend flavor and connotative authority to whatever is being said. There's not much more to say about the syntax of interjections than that.

# CHAPTER 12

# Concluding Remarks

*Cautions, provisos, and reservations*

Most of what has been presented here has been given as if it were absolute fact. Some of it is; but we need to bear in mind that language is at all times and places a plastic, evolving thing. Almost no rule or set of rules one can make about grammar, however simple or complex, will describe all validly grammatical utterances even within a given language. This conundrum is susceptible to exhaustive proof for at least mathematical systems of signification, but extending it from there to natural language is problematic and difficult; still, it seems likely (and informally validated by experience) that something like the same holds true of human language.

Even the most constrained and limited human language, in both complexity and capacity for nuance, dwarfs any purely logical system. Once one has accounted for the normal interplay of parts of speech, cases, phrases, and clauses, one can still fold into the mix such wild cards as irony and tonality, all of which complicate the matter further by several orders of magnitude. The universal human capacity for articulate speech is vast and prodigal; our propensity for complicating it and playing with it is even more so. It is probably not rigorously demonstrable, but virtually certain nonetheless, that every adult speaker of any language has, not once but many times, given voice to thoughts and phrases that are unique in the history of mankind. No one has ever said them before, and no one will ever say them again. We nevertheless appear to be at no risk of running out of new and (often) interesting things to say.

That being the case, therefore, it should not surprise anyone that no grammar of human language ever has been or ever will be complete. Even within a small community of speakers the permutations are too great, and the semantic need to express new ideas flexibly and precisely usually trumps any merely syntactical objections. Within a large community of speakers, and especially where those communities exist for a long time—as has been the case with Latin, Greek, and

English—the picture is further complicated by accidental or deliberate modification, change, and the human inclination to create and push back the boundaries of what is possible. Yesterday's solecism becomes today's standard diction. Shakespeare's adroit puns become everyone's standard quotations—and, more importantly, the foundation for further permutations.

One way of dealing with this is merely to admit defeat and move on to something else. But since such limitations will eventually hem in every other field of human endeavor as well, such concession must ultimately reduce us by destroying our aspirations. The human response—improbable, heroic, and ultimately doomed though it might be—is to struggle with the incomprehensible, and to battle against ignorance in others and especially in ourselves. Sometimes we make progress. Even if we don't win outright, we can arrive at a little better understanding of the nature of the problem, and we can learn a lot of fragmentary truths along the way.

Accordingly, what is in this book should be taken not as a set of hard and fast rules, but as a cautious (and sometimes perhaps incautious) sketch of the outline of how Greek and Latin work, with reference to English. It attempts to explain some of the dynamic relationships between them, and to allow a student, by comparing differences in approach and execution, to keep the facts at least largely straight so that he or she can move on to the more critical task of grappling with what people have had to say—in all the various subject areas they have addressed throughout the generations. This work is a jumping-off point, therefore: a point of entry into the larger literature of language scholarship and analysis. There is a huge body of such scholarship. I have attempted in the bibliography to suggest a few places in which you might like to pursue what is already known and what has been discovered on the subject. It is the merest sampling.

Ultimately, however, it is all just a means to a larger end. The responsibility for making sense of any text you confront does not reside with the historical community of grammarians and logicians of language; it rests with you. To approach any piece of writing with the respect it deserves, and the humility that befits any of us, requires that we seek to see both what is in the text and what is beyond it. We can examine modes of expression and diction, grammatical structures, and interesting case usage, but we also need to see *through* them to what the author was ultimately striving to express. To read a text is not merely to confront a collection of markings on a page, a range of syntactic constructions, or even a set of semantic signifiers; it is ultimately to encounter the person who wrote it. That person may be alive or may be dead, and so (in some sense) beyond the influence of our admiration or contempt, but if one undertakes that task seriously, merest courtesy must dictate that we do so with a sense of the gravity entailed in the encounter with anyone: that we not write anyone off without due consideration and without reserving at least the possibility that there is something more there than we initially might have suspected. An open reader cannot and must not ever completely close a text: There is always the possibility that it will have something further to say to us.

# Annotated Bibliography

*Resources for further study*

## English grammar

Burchfield, R. W. *Fowler's Modern English Usage*. Oxford: Oxford University Press, 2004.
This latest edition of a classic by H. W. Fowler (first published in 1926) has been widely praised and widely reviled, but it has a place in the library of anyone interested in grammar and usage in English. Fowler was a witty writer, and many of his articles are both entertaining and informative.

Curme, George O. *A Grammar of the English Language*. Old Lyme, Conn.: Verbatim Books, 1978.
Though out of print, this was one of the first attempts at an exhaustive linguist's grammar of the English language. It is in two volumes and runs to well over a thousand pages.

Greenbaum, Sidney. *Oxford English Grammar*. Oxford: Oxford University Press, 1996.
A standard and moderately prescriptive outline of basic English grammar. Its treatment of such things as the proper scope for the subjunctive is still rather incomplete, but it forms a reasonable foundation for almost any other grammatical investigation.

Quirk, Randolph, Sidney Greenbaum, Geoffrey Leech, and Jan Svartvik. *A Comprehensive Grammar of the English Language*. 2nd rev. ed. London: Longman, 1985.
This massive volume runs to nearly 1,800 pages and is probably the logical successor to Curme.

Warriner, John E. *English Grammar and Composition, Complete Course*. New York: Harcourt Brace, 1988.
Now out of print, this has remained for several generations the handbook of grammatical reference. It is neither the most complete nor the most accessible, but it is widely distributed, and copies are available used for a reasonable price.


## Latin grammar

Most of the books listed here are reprints of editions about a century old, and hence in the public domain. A variety of publishers have made modifications and revisions; some have done thorough overhauls, while others have made photo-re-productions of the original texts.

Allen, Joseph Henry, and James Bradstreet Greenough. *Allen and Greenough's New Latin Grammar*. Edited by G. L. Kittredge, A. A. Howard, Benj. L. D'Ooge, and Anne Mahoney. Newburyport, Mass.: Focus Publishing, 2001.
There are now many editions of this grammar available, as the original is now in the public domain, and any of them will provide virtually the same material. This work is widely regarded as the best standard reference grammar of the Latin language published in English. Professional scholars will still have recourse to the larger German volumes on Latin grammar, such as Leumann, Hofmann, and Szantyr, *Lateinische Grammatik*, but this grammar is solid. The version cited here has been cleaned up and rationalized recently by Anne Mahoney.

Bennett, Charles E., and Anne Mahoney. *New Latin Grammar*. Newburyport, Mass.: Focus Publishing, 2007.
Another standard and accessible English-language grammar of Latin.

Gildersleeve, Basil Lanneau, and Gonzales Lodge. *Gildersleeve's Latin Grammar*. Boston: D. C. Heath, 1894.
Another favorite intermediate-level reference grammar of the Latin language.

Grandgent, Charles Hall. *An Introduction to Vulgar Latin*. Boston: Heath, 1907.
Not the most recent but probably the most accessible discussion of the special subfield of Vulgar Latin (that is, the Latin of the *vulgus*—the common people) from antiquity onward. Still one of the better works available in English on the subject, though many of Grandgent's conclusions have been surpassed by Väänänen.

Hale, William Gardner, and Carl Darling Buck. *A Latin Grammar*. Boston: Athenaeum Press, 1903.
Buck was one of the first great Indo-Europeanists, and his grammar shows the influence of this connection.

Leumann, Manu, Friedrich Stolz, Hermann Bengtson, Johann Baptist Hofmann, Walter Otto, Iwan von Müller, and Anton Szantyr. *Lateinische Grammatik*. Munich: Beck, 1977.
As near as there is to a single comprehensive repository of Latin grammar. Written in German, containing abundant examples and exceptions of almost every variety. Probably not the best source for a normative grasp of Latin grammar, but the ultimate reference for documentation of a given form or usage. In three volumes, covering accidence, syntax, and other miscellany.

Mantello, Frank Anthony Carl, and A. G. Rigg. *Medieval Latin: An Introduction and Bibliographical Guide*. Washington, D.C.: Catholic University of America Press, 1996.
Not by any means a mere grammar, but a compendium of the various crossroads and background materials necessary for the reading of Medieval Latin, including grammatical and usage issues. An essential tool for anyone tackling the materials of Medieval Latin.

Väänänen, Veikko. *Introduction au Latin Vulgaire*. Paris: Klincksieck, 1967.
Probably the best currently available source on Vulgar Latin for those who can read French. Definitely a substantial improvement on Grandgent's introduction.

Woodcock, E. C. *A New Latin Syntax*. London: Methuen, 1959. Reprint, Wauconda, Ill.: Bolchazy-Carducci, 2005.
A revolutionary and unique look at Latin syntax from the ground up, seeing the whole as an integral system with an eye toward the historical linguistic considerations that lie behind each of the major systems and constructions it discusses. Indispensable for those seriously pursuing the kinds of questions this book attempts to raise.

## Greek grammar

Buck, Carl Darling. *Introduction to the Study of the Greek Dialects*. Boston: Ginn, 1910.
One of the relatively few unified discussions of the Greek dialects widely available in English. Contains introduction, grammatical notes, inscriptions, and text.

Denniston, John Dewar. *The Greek Particles*. Oxford: Oxford University Press, Second edition, 1954.
A spectacularly detailed and thorough discussion of the particles of the Greek language by one of the greatest grammarians of the twentieth century.

Goodwin, William Watson. *Greek Grammar*. Revised by Charles Burton Gulick. Boston: Ginn, ca. 1930.
A very solid discussion of Greek grammar from one of the better minds in the field, though perhaps not as accessible or as detailed as Smyth's.

———. *Syntax of the Moods and Tenses of the Greek Verb*. Boston: Ginn, 1897.
Goodwin, the author of the foregoing general grammar, here digs into the strange and wonderful mechanics of the Greek verb in special detail. The work has in some respects been surpassed in the intervening century, but Goodwin's overall view of the field is hard to equal; it contains a good deal that is valuable to the advanced student. It is not, however, particularly accessible: it is made up of gritty atomic detail from the very start.

Otto, Walter, Hermann Bengtson, Iwan von Müller, and Eduard Schwyzer. *Griechische Grammatik*. Munich: Beck, 1978.
A multivolume grammar of the Greek language in German, equivalent in scope to Leumann, Hofmann, and Szantyr's *Lateinische Grammatik*. The ultimate reference for Greek grammar, arguably, though like the Latin volumes, not immediately accessible even to the student with solid German skills, and inclined to support a lot of exceptions to the general rules.

Robertson, Archibald T. *A Grammar of the Greek New Testament in the Light of Historical Research*. New York: Hodder & Stoughton, 1914.
A substantial and meticulous investigation of the language specifically of the New Testament.

Smyth, Herbert Weir. *Greek Grammar.* Revised by Gordon M. Messing.
     Cambridge, Mass.: Harvard University Press, 1956.
     The leading grammar of the classical Greek language in English, this remains a
     monumental and exceedingly detailed account of the subject.


## Indo-European and comparative studies

*The American Heritage Dictionary of the English Language.* 4th ed. Boston:
     Houghton Mifflin Harcourt, 2006.
     This is a solid dictionary in its own right, but it is particularly interesting for
     the student of Latin and Greek because it contains a very valuable appendix of
     Indo-European roots, which discusses how those are manifested in a variety
     of different Indo-European languages. The appendix has been published sep-
     arately as well.

Buck, Carl Darling. *A Comparative Grammar of Greek and Latin.* Chicago:
     University of Chicago Press, 1969.
     Concentrating more on morphology than syntax, nevertheless a very valuable
     contribution to the study of comparative grammar.

————. *A Dictionary of Selected Synonyms in the Principal Indo-European
     Languages.* 1949. Reprint, Chicago: University of Chicago Press, 1988.
     Lexical comparisons across a variety of languages concentrating chiefly on
     morphology.

Moore, R. W. *Comparative Greek and Latin Syntax.* London: G. Bell and Sons,
     1934.
     A remarkably penetrating study of the syntactical commonalities and differ-
     ences between Greek and Latin, well ahead of its time.

Sihler, Andrew L. *New Comparative Grammar of Greek and Latin.* Oxford:
     Oxford University Press, 1995.
     Much more modern than Buck's comparative grammar, this book contains
     much of the latest research in the subject. Like Buck, however, it is primarily
     morphological in focus.

# Index

ablative, 126; absent from Greek, 127;
  absolute, in Latin, 151; cause, in Latin,
  148; compared with accusative, 126;
  personal agent, in Latin, 150; physical
  referent, 127; respect, in Latin, 147–48
absolute construction, 151; ambiguity in,
  152; separative, 152–53
absolute versus relative time, in Greek
  tenses, 102
abstract nouns, in Classical and Medieval
  Latin, 158
accent change, in Greek, 87
accusative, 129–30; adverbial, in Greek,
  149; direct object, 138; goal of motion,
  129; limit of space or time, 130;
  respect, in Greek, 148
accusative-infinitive indirect statement:
  in Greek, 77; in Latin, 72
active voice, 113–14
actual result, in Greek, 36
adjectival clause, 29–30, 54–62
adjective, 8, 119; demonstrative, 11, 171–
  78; interrogative, 10, 185; possessive,
  178; pronoun, 10; substantivized, 8
advantage or disadvantage, dative, 146
adverb, 14; function of, 14, 16; limiting
  scope of predication, 33; in sentence,
  15; variety of uses, 15

adverbial accusative, in Greek, 149
adverbial clause, 29, 30, 32–53; answering
  question, 33; types of, 32
adverbial relative clause, 49
agency, with passive verbs, 115–16, 150
agent, dative, 146
antecedent of pronoun, 10
aorist, 97; aspect, in Latin, 98; gnomic,
  102; versus perfect aspect, in Latin,
  98, 100; and perfect fusion, in Latin,
  98; as snapshot, 101; system, 93
apodosis, 40; variation in, 47
Aristotle, logical writings of, 20
article, 11, 189; defining attributive
  position, in Greek, 191; definite, in
  English, 12, 189; as demonstrative
  pronoun, in Greek, 173–74; in Greek,
  12, 190, 191; indefinite, in English 12;
  lacking, in Latin, 190; as pronoun, in
  Greek, 13; in Romance languages, 191
articular infinitive, in Greek, 13, 112, 113,
  156
aspect, 37, 91–95; adverbial marking, 97;
  in English, 92; relating events, 92, 97–
  98; simple, 92; and tense, 91–102; and
  tense, in Greek moods and verbals,
  101–102
attributive position, in Greek, 12

case, 119, 122–23, 124 (*fig.*); development, 130–31; in English, 123–24; in English, Latin, and Proto-Indo-European, 124–30; reduction, in Latin and Greek, 124
causal constructions, 148–49
causation, 33–34
Centum languages, 84, 85 (*fig.*); 90
Cicero, 98–99
Classical Greek versus Koine Greek, 107
clause, 24; adverbial, 32–53; causal, 33–34; comparative, 50–51; concessive, 48; conditional, 37- 44; dependent, 25–26; exclamatory, 52–53; independent, 25–26; manner, 49; place, 49; purpose, 33–35; result, 33, 35; temporal, 36–40; types, 24
cognate accusative, 150
collective nouns, number, 121
command, indirect. *See* indirect command
comparative clause, 50–51
comparison, 136; and condition, 50; Greek, genitive, 136; Latin, ablative, 136; quantity or degree, 51; separative concept, 136
complex sentence, 27–28
compound sentence, 27
conative imperfect, 95
concessive clause, 48
condition, 37–47; clause, 37, 40–44; contrary-to-fact, 41–44; future, in Latin and Greek, 44–46; general versus particular, 41; Greek, 46 (*fig.*); Latin, 47 (*fig.*); and temporal clause, related to, 40; variation, in apodosis, 47
conditional relative clause, 60–61
conditional sentence, 37, 47
conjunction, 17, 193–94
connecting relative pronoun, 61–62
contents, genitive, 144
contingency, 36; in future and subjunctive, 105; and time, 3
contrary-to-fact condition, 41–44
copula, 14, 22; implied, 23
correlative pronouns, 188

dative, 128–29; advantage or disadvantage, 146; agent, 146–47; ethical, 146; indirect object, 138; lexical variations, 138; possession, 142; respect, 146
definite article, in English, 12, 189
demonstrative adjective and pronoun, 11, 171–78; article as, in Greek, 173–74; persons, 175–77; strong, 174–78; weak, 171–74
dependent clause, 25–26
deponent verbs, 118
determinacy, in temporal clause, 37
direct object, 138; outgrowth of motion, 129
divided whole. *See* partitive
dual, 90–91, 120–21

emphatic verbs, in English, 93
enduring consequence, of perfect, 96
epithet, 8
ethical dative, 146
exclamatory clause and phrase, 52–53
existential use of state-of-being verb, 14, 23–24
extent of space, accusative, 134
extent of time, accusative, 135

finite moods, 103
future active participle, purpose of, 164
future condition, particularity of, 44. *See also under* condition
future participle, 164
future passive participle, in Latin, 164
future tense, 94

manner, 137; clause, 49

mass nouns: poetic use, 121–22; number, 121

material, genitive, 144

means, or instrument, 137

measure, genitive, 144–45

middle voice, 113, 117–18

mood, in verbs, 89, 103–109

motion, with prepositions, in Latin, 141

natural result, in Greek, 36

nominative, 125

noun, 4–9, 119–53; common versus proper, 4–5; concrete versus abstract, 6–7; marking, 119; substantive versus adjective, 7–8

noun clause, 29, 63–83; as appositive, 65; fearing or striving, 64–65; pseudoclauses, 63; subject or object, 29, 63

number, 119–22; in mass or collective nouns, 121; in verbs, 89–90

object: direct, 138; indirect, 138; of preposition, 139–42; of verb, 114

objective genitive, 143–44

obligation and necessity, Latin gerundive, 164

optative mood, in Greek, 106–107

*oratio obliqua. See* indirect discourse

parenthetical relative clause. *See* relative clause, restrictive versus nonrestrictive

participial indirect statement, in Greek, 77

participial phrase, in Greek: semantic burden, 165; resembling clause, 63

participle, 113, 154, 158–68; dangling, in English, 162–63; in English, 159; in Greek, 165–68; in Latin, 163–64; misidentified, in English, 160

particle, 4, 18, 191–92

partitive genitive, 142, 144–45

parts of sentence, 19–31; alternative terminology, 19

parts of speech, 3 (*fig.*); eight, 3; functions, 3–4

passive voice, 113–16; agent with, 150

pejorative demonstrative, 177

perfect aspect, 95–96, 98

perfect passive verbs, formation and meaning, 100

perfect system, 93, 95

perfect tenses, 91

person, definition of, 90; in verbs, 89–90

personal agent, 150

personal pronoun, 170–71; genitive, possession, in Greek, 180; oblique cases of, 171; third person, lacking, in Greek and Latin, 171

personal source, 134

persons, of demonstrative pronoun, 175–77

phrases, distinguished from clauses, 31

place constructions, 49; from which, 132; to which, 133; where, 133

plural, 120

possession, 142–43

possessive pronoun and adjective, 178–80; substantivized, 179

predicate, 19–22

predicate nominative, implicit, 125

predication: action versus state-of-being, 22; philosophical terms, 20–21

preposition, 16, 192; in Greek, 142 (*fig.*); in Latin, 140 (*fig.*); object, cases, 139–41; origins and functions, as adverb, 16–17, 139

prepositional phrase, in Greek, and adjectival force, 192

present tense, 94

preterite, 97

price or value, genitive, 144–45